Thornton Wilder
Our Town

Thornton Wilder **Our Town**

Herausgegeben von:
Patrick Charles

Verlagsredaktion:
Neil Porter

Gestaltung & technische Umsetzung:
Anna Bakalović und Annika Preyhs, Berlin

Umschlagillustrationen:
Großes Bild: © Joseph Sohm; Visions of America/CORBIS
Kleines Bild: © Judy Griesedieck/CORBIS

Herausgeber der Cornelsen Senior English Library:
Prof. Dr. Albert-Reiner Glaap

www.cornelsen.de

1. Auflage, 1. Druck 2005

Alle Drucke dieser Auflage sind inhaltlich unverändert
und können im Unterricht nebeneinander verwendet werden.

© 2005 Cornelsen Verlag, Berlin

Druck: CS-Druck CornelsenStürtz, Berlin

ISBN-13: 978-3-464-31086-1
ISBN-10:   3-464-31086-8

Inhalt gedruckt auf säurefreiem Papier,
umweltschonend hergestellt aus chlorfrei gebleichten Faserstoffen.

Contents

Abbreviations and Annotations

adj	adjective	**infml**	informal
adv	adverb	**jdm/jdn**	jemandem/en
AE	American English	**n**	noun
cf.	confer; see	**p., pp.**	page, pages
derog	derogatory	**pl**	plural
e.g.	exempli gratia; for example	**sb.**	somebody
esp.	especially	**sl**	slang
etc.	et cetera; and so on	**sth.**	something
fml	formal	**usu.**	usually
i.e.	id est; in other words	**v**	verb

The annotations are arranged chronologically; the first time a word is used is where you will find it explained. All pronunciations given are American English.

For help about reading and presenting literature in the classroom, cf. **www.learnetix.de/bookshelf**.

The Characters

(in order of appearance)

Stage Manager
Dr. Gibbs
Joe Crowell
Howie Newsome
Mrs. Gibbs
Mrs. Webb
George Gibbs
Wally Webb
Emily Webb
Professor Willard
Mr. Webb
Woman in the Balcony
Man in the Auditorium
Lady in the Box
Simon Stimson
Mrs. Soames
Constable Warren
Si Crowell
Baseball Players
Sam Craig
Joe Stoddard
People of the Town

The entire play takes place in Grover's Corner, New Hampshire, 1901 to 1913.

First performance, January 22, 1938

Act I

No curtain.

No scenery.

The audience, arriving, sees an empty stage in half-light.

Presently the STAGE MANAGER, *hat on and pipe in mouth, enters and begins*
5 *placing a table and three chairs downstage left, and a table and three chairs*
downstage right.

He also places a low bench at the corner of what will be the Webb house, left.
"Left" and "right" are from the point of view of the actor facing the audience.
"Up" is toward the back wall.

10 *As the house lights go down he has finished setting the stage and leaning*
against the right proscenium pillar watches the late arrivals in the audience.
When the auditorium is in complete darkness he speaks:

STAGE MANAGER: This play is called "Our Town." It was written by
Thornton Wilder; produced and directed by A. ... (or: produced by
15 A. ...; directed by B. ...). In it you will see Miss C. ...; Miss D. ...;
Miss E. ...; and Mr. F. ...; Mr. G. ...; Mr. H. ...; and many others. The
name of the town is Grover's Corners, New Hampshire – just across
the Massachusetts line: latitude 42 degrees 40 minutes; longitude 70
degrees 37 minutes. The first Act shows a day in our town. The day
20 is May 7, 1901. The time is just before dawn.

A rooster crows.

The sky is beginning to show some streaks of light over in the East
there, behind our mount'in.

The morning star always gets wonderful bright the minute before it
25 has to go, – doesn't it?

He stares at it for a moment, then goes upstage.

Well, I'd better show you how our town lies. Up here –

---

11 **proscenium** [proʊ'siːniəm]: arch that separates a stage from the audience
21 **rooster** (AE): male chicken   23 **mount'in** (non-standard pron): mountain

That is: parallel with the back wall.

is Main Street. Way back there is the railway station; tracks go that way. Polish Town's across the tracks, and some Canuck families.

Toward the left.

Over there is the Congregational Church; across the street's the   5
Presbyterian.

Methodist and Unitarian are over there.

Baptist is down in the holla' by the river.

Catholic Church is over beyond the tracks.

Here's the Town Hall and Post Office combined; jail's in the   10
basement.

Bryan once made a speech from these very steps here.

Along here's a row of stores. Hitching posts and horse blocks in front of them. First automobile's going to come along in about five years – belonged to Banker Cartwright, our richest citizen ... lives in the   15
big white house up on the hill.

Here's the grocery store and here's Mr. Morgan's drugstore. Most everybody in town manages to look into those two stores once a day.

Public School's over yonder. High School's still farther over. Quarter   20
of nine mornings, noontimes, and three o'clock afternoons, the hull town can hear the yelling and screaming from those schoolyards.

He approaches the table and chairs downstage right.

This is our doctor's house, – Doc Gibbs'. This is the back door.

Two arched trellises, covered with vines and flowers, are pushed out, one by   25
each proscenium pillar.

There's some scenery for those who think they have to have scenery.

This is Mrs. Gibbs' garden. Corn ... peas ... beans ... hollyhocks ... heliotrope ... and a lot of burdock.

Crosses the stage.
                                                                          30

In those days our newspaper come out twice a week – the Grover's Corners *Sentinel* – and this is Editor Webb's house.

And this is Mrs. Webb's garden.

Just like Mrs. Gibbs', only it's got a lot of sunflowers, too.

35 *He looks upward, center stage.*

Right here …'s a big butternut tree.

He returns to his place by the right proscenium pillar and looks at the audience for a minute.

Nice town, y'know what I mean?

40 Nobody very remarkable ever come out of it, s'far as we know.

The earliest tombstones in the cemetery up there on the mountain say 1670–1680 – they're Grovers and Cartwrights and Gibbses and Herseys – same names as are around here now.

Well, as I said: it's about dawn.

45 The only lights on in town are in a cottage over by the tracks where a Polish mother's just had twins. And in the Joe Crowell house, where Joe Junior's getting up so as to deliver the paper. And in the depot, where Shorty Hawkins is gettin' ready to flag the 5:45 for Boston.

A train whistle is heard. The STAGE MANAGER *takes out his watch and nods.*

---

2 **tracks**: Eisenbahngleise   3 **Canuck** (AE sl): Canadians, esp. French-Canadians
5–8 **Congregational Church, Presbyterian, Methodist, Baptist**: various Protestant
denominations (= Glaubensgemeinschaften)   7 **Unitarian**: Protestant denomination
that rejects belief in the Trinity (= die Heilige Dreifaltigkeit)   9 **holla'** (non-standard
pron) = **hollow**: small valley   12 **William Jenkins Bryan** (1860–1925): politician
who gained a reputation for travelling the country delivering speeches   13 **hitching
post**: post used for tying up horses   **horse block**: piece of wood used for climbing
onto horses   20 **over yonder**: over there   21 **hull** (non-standard pron): whole
25 **trellis**: wooden climbing frame for plants   28–29 **hollyhock, heliotrope,
burdock**: types of plants   36 **butternut tree** (AE): walnut tree   47 **depot** ['di:poʊ]
(AE): railway station   48 **flag sth.**: (formerly) stop sth. (esp. a train) by using a flag
as a signal to a train driver

Naturally, out in the country – all around – there've been lights on for some time, what with milkin's and so on. But town people sleep late.

So – another day's begun.

There's Doc Gibbs comin' down Main Street now, comin' back from 5 that baby case. And here's his wife comin' downstairs to get breakfast.

MRS. GIBBS, *a plump, pleasant woman in the middle thirties, comes "downstairs" right. She pulls up an imaginary window shade in her kitchen and starts to make a fire in her stove.* 10

Doc Gibbs died in 1930. The new hospital's named after him.

Mrs. Gibbs died first – long time ago, in fact. She went out to visit her daughter, Rebecca, who married an insurance man in Canton, Ohio, and died there – pneumonia – but her body was brought back here. She's up in the cemetery there now – in with a whole mess of 15 Gibbses and Herseys – she was Julia Hersey 'fore she married Doc Gibbs in the Congregational Church over there.

In our town we like to know the facts about everybody.

There's Mrs. Webb, coming downstairs to get her breakfast, too.

– That's Doc Gibbs. Got that call at half past on this morning. 20

And there comes Joe Crowell, Jr., delivering Mr. Webb's *Sentinel*.

DR. GIBBS *has been coming along Main Street from the left. At the point where he would turn to approach his house, he stops, sets down his – imaginary – black bag, takes off his hat, and rubs his face with fatigue, using an enormous handkerchief.* 25

MRS. WEBB, *a thin, serious, crisp woman, has entered her kitchen, left, tying on an apron. She goes through the motions of putting wood into a stove, lighting it, and preparing breakfast.*

Suddenly, JOE CROWELL, JR., *eleven, starts down Main Street from the right, hurling imaginary newspapers into doorways.* 30

JOE CROWELL, JR.: Morning, Doc Gibbs,

DR. GIBBS: Morning, Joe.

JOE CROWELL, JR.: Somebody been sick, Doc?

DR. GIBBS: No. Just some twins born over in Polish Town.

35 **JOE CROWELL, JR.**: Do you want your paper now?

DR. GIBBS: Yes, I'll take it. – Anything serious goin' on in the world since Wednesday?

JOE CROWELL, JR.: Yessir. My schoolteacher, Miss Foster, 's getting married to a fella over in Concord.

40 **DR. GIBBS**: I declare. – How do you boys feel about that?

JOE CROWELL, JR.: Well, of course, it's none of my business – but I think if a person starts out to be a teacher, she ought to stay one.

DR. GIBBS: How's your knee, Joe?

JOE CROWELL, JR.: Fine, Doc, I never think about it at all. Only like you
45 said, it always tells me when it's going to rain.

DR. GIBBS: What's it telling you today? Goin' to rain?

JOE CROWELL, JR.: No, sir.

DR. GIBBS: Sure?

JOE CROWELL, JR.: Yessir.

50 **DR. GIBBS**: Knee ever make a mistake?

JOE CROWELL, JR.: No, sir.

JOE *goes off.* DR. GIBBS *stands reading his paper.*

STAGE MANAGER: Want to tell you something about that boy Joe
Crowell there. Joe was awful bright – graduated from high school
55 here, head of his class. So he got a scholarship to Massachusetts Tech.
Graduated head of his class there, too. It was all wrote up in the
Boston paper at the time. Goin' to be a great engineer, Joe was. But

---

14 **pneumonia** [nu'mouniə]: Lungenentzündung   15 **a whole mess of** (AE sl):
(here) a lot of   30 **hurl sth.**: throw sth.   39 **fella**: fellow   40 **I declare**: (here)
expression of surprise   54–55 **graduate head of your class**: leave school with the
best marks in your class   56 **wrote up** (non-standard): written about

the war broke out and he died in France. – All that education for nothing.

HOWIE NEWSOME: *[Off left.]* Giddap, Bessie! What's the matter with you today?

STAGE MANAGER: Here comes Howie Newsome, deliverin' the milk.   5

HOWIE NEWSOME, *about thirty, in overalls, comes along Main Street from the left, walking beside an invisible horse and wagon and carrying an imaginary rack with milk bottles. The sound of clinking milk bottles is heard. He leaves some bottles at Mrs. Webb's trellis, then, crossing the stage to Mrs. Gibbs', he stops center to talk to Dr. Gibbs.*   10

HOWIE NEWSOME: Morning, Doc.

DR. GIBBS: Morning, Howie.

HOWIE NEWSOME: Somebody sick?

DR. GIBBS: Pair of twins over to Mrs. Goruslawski's.

HOWIE NEWSOME: Twins, eh? This town's gettin' bigger every year.   15

DR. GIBBS: Goin' to rain, Howie?

HOWIE NEWSOME: No, no. Fine day – that'll burn through. Come on, Bessie.

DR. GIBBS: Hello Bessie.

He strokes the horse, which has remained up center.   20

DR. GIBBS: How old is she, Howie?

HOWIE NEWSOME: Going on seventeen. Bessie's all mixed up about the route ever since the Lockharts stopped takin' their quart of milk every day. She wants to leave 'em a quart just the same – keeps scolding me the hull trip.   25

He reaches Mrs. Gibbs' back door. She is waiting for him.

DR. GIBBS: Good morning, Howie.

HOWIE NEWSOME: Morning, Mrs. Gibbs. Doc's just comin' down the street.

MRS. GIBBS: Is he? Seems like you're late today.   30

HOWIE NEWSOME: Yes. Somep'n went wrong with the separator. Don't know what 'twas.

He passes DR. GIBBS *up center.*

Doc!

35 **DR. GIBBS:** Howie!

MRS. GIBBS: *[Calling upstairs.]* Children! Children! Time to get up.

HOWIE NEWSOME: Come on, Bessie!

He goes off right.

MRS. GIBBS: George! Rebecca!

40 DR. GIBBS *arrives at his back door and passes through the trellis into his house.*

MRS. GIBBS: Everything all right, Frank?

DR. GIBBS: Yes. I declare – easy as kittens.

MRS. GIBBS: Bacon'll be ready in a minute. Set down and drink your
45 coffee. You can catch a couple hours' sleep this morning, can't you?

DR. GIBBS: Hm! … Mrs. Wentworth's coming at eleven. Guess I know what it's about, too. Her stummick ain't what it ought to be.

MRS. GIBBS: All told, you won't get more'n three hours' sleep. Frank Gibbs, I don't know what's goin' to become of you. I do wish I could
50 get you to go away someplace and take a rest. I think it would do you good.

MRS. WEBB: Emileeee! Time to get up! Wally! Seven o'clock!

MRS. GIBBS: I declare, you got to speak to George. Seems like something's come over him lately. He's no help to me at all. I can't even get him to
55 cut me some wood.

---

3 **giddap**: noise made to a horse to make it start moving   6 **overalls** (pl): work
clothes   17 **burn through**: the sun will shine   23 **quart** (AE): unit of measurement
(ca. 0,95 l)   25 **scold sb.**: jdn. ausschimpfen   31 **somep'n** (non-standard pron):
something   **separator**: dairy machine   44 **set down** (non-standard pron): sit
down   47 **stummick** (non-standard pron): stomach   48 **all told**: alles in allem

DR. GIBBS: *[Washing and drying his hands at the sink.* MRS. GIBBS *is busy at the stove.]* Is he sassy to you?

MRS. GIBBS: No. He just whines! All he thinks about is that baseball – George! Rebecca! You'll be late for school.

DR. GIBBS: M-m-m …   5

MRS. GIBBS: George!

DR. GIBBS: George, look sharp!

GEORGE'S VOICE: Yes, Pa!

DR. GIBBS: *[As he goes off the stage.]* Don't you hear your mother calling you? I guess I'll go upstairs and get forty winks.   10

MRS. WEBB: Walleee! Emileee! You'll be late for school! Walleee! You wash yourself good or I'll come up and do it myself.

REBECCA GIBBS' VOICE: Ma! What dress shall I wear?

MRS. GIBBS: Don't make a noise: Your father's been out all night and needs his sleep. I washed and ironed the blue gingham for you   15 special.

REBECCA: Ma, I hate that dress.

MRS. GIBBS: Oh, hush-up-with-you.

REBECCA: Every day I go to school dressed like a sick turkey.

MRS. GIBBS: Now, Rebecca, you always look *very* nice.   20

REBECCA: Mama, Goerge's throwing soap at me.

MRS. GIBBS: I'll come and slap the both of you, – that's what I'll do.

A factory whistle sounds.

The Children dash in and take their places at the tables. Right, GEORGE, *about sixteen, and* REBECCA, *eleven. Left,* EMILY *and* WALLY, *same ages. They carry*   25 *strapped schoolbooks.*

STAGE MANAGER: We've got a factory in our town too – hear it? Makes blankets. Cartwrights own it and it brung 'em a fortune.

MRS. WEBB: Children! Now I won't have it. Breakfast is just as good as
30   any other meal and I won't have you gobbling like wolves. It'll stunt
        your growth, – that's a fact. Put away your book, Wally.

WALLY: Aw, Ma! By ten o'clock I got to know all about Canada.

MRS. WEBB: You know the rule's well as I do – no books at table. As for
        me, I'd rather have my children healthy than bright.

35   EMILY: I'm both, Mama: you know I am. I'm the brightest girl in school
        for my age. I have a wonderful memory.

MRS. WEBB: Eat your breakfast.

WALLY: I'm bright, too, when I'm looking at my stamp collection.

MRS. GIBBS: I'll speak to your father about it when he's rested. Seems to
40   me twenty-five cents a week's enough for a boy your age. I declare I
        don't know how you spend it all.

GEORGE: Aw, Ma, – I gotta lotta things to buy.

MRS. GIBBS: Strawberry phosphates – that's what you spend it on.

GEORGE: I don't see how Rebecca comes to have so much money. She
45   has more'n a dollar.

REBECCA: [Spoon in mouth, dreamily.] I've been saving it up gradual.

MRS. GIBBS: Well, dear, I think it's a good thing to spend some every
        now and then.

REBECCA: Mama, do you know what I love most in the world – do you?
50   – Money.

MRS. GIBBS: Eat your breakfast.

---

2 **sassy** (AE): frech   3 **whine**: jammern   7 **look sharp!**: (here) hurry up!
10 **forty winks**: a little sleep   15 **gingham**: Gingan (Baumwollstoff)   18 **hush-up-with-you** (AE): be quiet   22 **slap sb.**: jdm. eine Ohrfeige geben   26 **strapped**:
bound together   28 **brung** (non-standard): brought   30 **gobble**: eat too fast
30–31 **stunt your growth**: stop you from growing   34 **bright**: clever   42 **lotta**
(non-standard): a lot of   43 **phosphate**: type of carbonated drink   46 **gradual**:
gradually, slowly

THE CHILDREN: Mama, there's first bell. – I gotta hurry. – I don't want any more. – I gotta hurry.

The Children rise, seize their books and dash out through the trellises. They meet, down center, and chattering, walk to Main Street, then turn left.

The STAGE MANAGER *goes off, unobtrusively, right.*   5

MRS. WEBB: Walk fast, but you don't have to run. Wally, pull up your pants at the knee. Stand up straight, Emily.

MRS. GIBBS: Tell Miss Foster I send her my best congratulations – can you remember that?

REBECCA: Yes, Ma.   10

MRS. GIBBS: You look real nice, Rebecca. Pick up your feet.

ALL: Good-by.

MRS. GIBBS *fills her apron with food for the chickens and comes down to the footlights.*

MRS. GIBBS: Here, chick, chick, chick.   15

No, go away, you. Go away.

Here, chick, chick, chick.

What's the matter with *you*? Fight, fight, fight, – that's all you do.

Hm … *you* don't belong to me. Where'd you come from?

She shakes her apron.   20

Oh, don't be so scared. Nobody's going to hurt you.

MRS. WEBB *is sitting on the bench by her trellis, stringing beans.*

Good morning, Myrtle. How's your cold?

MRS. WEBB: Well, I still get that tickling feeling in my throat. I told Charles I didn't know as I'd go to choir practice tonight. Wouldn't be   25 any use.

MRS. GIBBS: Have you tried singing over your voice?

MRS. WEBB: Yes, but somehow I can't do that and stay on the key. While I'm resting myself I thought I'd string some of these beans.

30   **MRS. GIBBS:** *[Rolling up her sleeves as she crosses the stage for a chat.]* Let me help you. Beans have been good this year.

MRS. WEBB: I've decided to put up forty quarts if it kills me. The children say they hate 'em, but I notice they're able to get 'em down all winter.

35   *Pause. Brief sound of chickens cackling.*

MRS. GIBBS: Now, Myrtle. I've got to tell you something, because if I don't tell somebody I'll burst.

MRS. WEBB: Why, Julia Gibbs!

MRS. GIBBS: Here, give me some more of those beans. Myrtle, did one of
40   those secondhand-furniture men from Boston come to see you last Friday?

MRS. WEBB: No—o.

MRS. GIBBS: Well, he called on me. First I thought he was a patient wantin' to see Dr. Gibbs. 'N he wormed his way into my parlor, and,
45   Myrtle Webb, he offered me three hundred and fifty dollars for Grandmother Wentworth's highboy, as I'm sitting here!

MRS. WEBB: Why, Julia Gibbs!

MRS. GIBBS: He did! That old thing! Why, it was so big I didn't know where to put it and I almost give it to Cousin Hester Wilcox.

50   **MRS. WEBB:** Well, you're going to take it, aren't you?

MRS. GIBBS: I don't know.

MRS. WEBB: You don't know – three hundred and fifty dollars! What's come over you?

---

5 **unobtrusively**: unauffällig   14 **footlights**: lights at the front of the stage
22 **string beans**: Bohnen putzen   25 **as I'd go** (non-standard): if I'd go   27 **sing
over your voice**: sing so as to avoid using certain parts of the throat   28 **stay on
key**: keep singing in tune   32 **put sth. up**: conserve sth.; make stores of sth.
33 **get 'em down**: eat them   44 **worm your way into sth.**: sich in etwas
hineinschleichen   46 **highboy** (AE): tall cupboard   **as I'm sitting here!**: just like
that!

MRS. GIBBS: Well, if I could get the Doctor to take the money and go away someplace on a real trip, I'd sell it like that. – Y'know, Myrtle, it's been the dream of my life to see Paris, France. – Oh, I don't know. It sounds crazy, I suppose, but for years I've been promising myself that if we ever had the chance –   5

MRS. WEBB: How does the Doctor feel about it?

MRS. GIBBS: Well, I did beat about the bush a little and said that if I got a legacy – that's the way I put it – I'd make him take me somewhere.

MRS. WEBB: M–m–m … What did he say?

MRS. GIBBS: You know how he is. I haven't heard a serious word out of   10 him since I've known him. No, he said, it might make him discontented with Grover's Corners to go traipsin' about Europe; better let well enough alone, he says. Every two years he makes a trip to the battlefields of the Civil War and that's enough treat for anybody, he says.   15

MRS. WEBB: Well, Mr. Webb just *admires* the way Dr. Gibbs knows everything about the Civil War. Mr. Webb's a good mind to give up Napoleon and move over to the Civil War, only Dr. Gibbs being one of the greatest experts in the country just makes him despair.

MRS. GIBBS: It's a fact! Dr. Gibbs is never so happy as when he's at   20 Antietam or Gettysburg. The times I've walked over those hills, Myrtle, stopping at every bush and pacing it all out, like we were going to buy it.

MRS. WEBB: Well, if that secondhand man's really serious about buyin' it, Julia, you sell it. And then you'll get to see Paris, all right. Just   25 keep droppin' hints from time to time – that's how I got to see the Atlantic Ocean, y'know.

MRS. GIBBS: Oh, I'm sorry I mentioned it. Only it seems to me that once in your life before you die you ought to see a country where they don't talk in English and don't even want to.   30

The STAGE MANAGER *enters briskly from the right. He tips his hat to the ladies, who nod their heads.*

STAGE MANAGER: Thank you, ladies. Thank you very much.

MRS. GIBBS *and* MRS. WEBB *gather up their things, return into their homes and*
35 *disappear.*

Now we're going to skip a few hours.

But first we want a little more information about the town, kind of a
scientific account, you might say.

So I've asked Professor Willard of our State University to sketch in a
40 few details of our past history here.

Is Professor Willard here?

PROFESSOR WILLARD, *a rural savant, pince-nez on a wide satin ribbon, enters
from the right with some notes in his hand.*

May I introduce Professor Willard of our State University.

45 A few brief notes, thank you, Professor, – unfortunately our time is
limited.

PROFESSOR WILLARD: Grover's Corners ... let me see ... Grover's
Corners lies on the old Pleistocene granite of the Appalachian range.
I may say it's some of the oldest land in the world. We're very proud
50 of that. A shelf of Devonian basalt crosses it with vestiges of Mesozoic
shale, and some sandstone outcroppings; but that's all more recent:
two hundred, three hundred million years old.

Some highly interesting fossils have been found ... I may say: unique
fossils ... two miles out of town, in Silas Peckham's cow pasture.
55 They can be seen at the museum in our University at any time – that
is, at any reasonable time. Shall I read some of Professor Gruber's

---

7 **beat about the bush**: not talk directly about sth.   8 **legacy**: Erbschaft
12 **traipse about sth.** (infml): wander around sth.   13 **better let well enough
alone** (AE): it's better to leave things as they are   17 **have a good mind to do sth.**:
seriously consider doing sth.   21 **Antietam, Gettysburg**: sites of famous battles
in the American Civil War   26 **drop hints**: Andeutungen machen   31 **briskly**:
quickly   42 **rural savant** [sə'vɑːnt]: ländlicher Gelehrter   **pince-nez**: Kneifer
(bügellose Brille)   48 **Pleistocene**: (geologisches Ära) Pleistozän   **Appalachian
range**: mountains in the east of the USA   50 **basalt**: volcanic rock   **vestiges**:
remains   51 **shale**: Schiefer   **outcroppings**: Felsen   54 **pasture**: field where
animals eat

notes on the meteorological situation – mean precipitation, et cetera?

STAGE MANAGER: Afraid we won't have time for that, Professor. We might have a few words on the history of man here.

PROFESSOR WILLARD: Yes ... anthropological data: Early Amerindian 5 stock. Cotahatchee tribes ... no evidence before the tenth century of this era ... hm ... now entirely disappeared ... possible traces in three families. Migration toward the end of the seventeenth century of English brachiocephalic blue-eyed stock ... for the most part. Since then some Slav and Mediterranean – 10

STAGE MANAGER: And the population, Professor Willard?

PROFESSOR WILLARD: Within the town limits: 2,640.

STAGE MANAGER: Just a moment, Professor.

He whispers into the professor's ear.

PROFESSOR WILLARD: Oh, yes, indeed? – The population, *at the* 15 *moment,* is 2,642. The Postal District brings in 507 more, making a total of 3,149. – Mortality and birth rates: constant. – By MacPherson's gauge: 6.032.

STAGE MANAGER: Thank you very much, Professor. We're all very much obliged to you, I'm sure. 20

PROFESSOR WILLARD: Not at all, sir; not at all.

STAGE MANAGER: This way, Professor, and thank you again.

Exit PROFESSOR WILLARD.

Now the political and social report: Editor Webb. – Oh, Mr. Webb?

MRS. WEBB *appears at her back door.* 25

MRS. WEBB: He'll be here in a minute. ... He just cut his hand while he was eatin' an apple.

STAGE MANAGER: Thank you, Mrs. Webb.

MRS. WEBB: Charles! Everybody's waitin'.

Exit MRS. WEBB. 30

STAGE MANAGER: Mr. Webb is Publisher and editor of the *Grover's Corners Sentinel*. That's our local paper, y'know.

MR. WEBB *enters from his house, pulling on his coat. His finger is bound in a handkerchief.*

35 **MR. WEBB:** Well … I don't have to tell you that we're run here by a Board of Selectmen. – All males vote at the age of twenty-one. Women vote indirect. We're lower middle class: sprinkling of professional men … ten per cent illiterate laborers. Politically, we're eighty-six per cent Republicans; six per cent Democrats; four per cent Socialists; 40 rest, indifferent.

Religiously, we're eighty-five per cent Protestants, twelve per cent Catholics; rest, indifferent.

STAGE MANAGER: Have you any comments, Mr. Webb?

MR. WEBB: Very ordinary town, if you ask me. Little better behaved than 45 most. Probably a lot duller.

But our young people here seem to like it well enough. Ninety per cent of 'em graduating from high school settle down right here to live – even when they've been away to college.

STAGE MANAGER: Now, is there anyone in the audience who would like 50 to ask Editor Webb anything about the town?

WOMAN IN THE BALCONY: Is there much drinking in Grover's Corners?

MR. WEBB: Well, ma'am, I wouldn't know what you'd call *much*. Satiddy nights the farmhands meet down in Ellery Greenough's stable and 55 holler some. We've got one or two town drunks, but they're always

---

1 **mean precipitation**: average rainfall   5 **Amerindian**: Native American
6 **stock**: Abstammung   9 **brachiocephalic**: kurzschädelig   17 **mortality and birth rates**: Sterblichkeits- und Geburtenraten   18 **gauge [geɪdʒ]**: measurement
20 **obliged to sb.**: be grateful to sb.   36 **Board of Selectmen** (AE): Gemeinderat
37 **a sprinkling**: (here) a few   38 **illiterate**: unable to read and write
40 **indifferent**: having no opinion; not interested in sth.   45 **dull**: not very interesting   53 **Satiddy** (non-standard pron): Saturday   54 **farmhand**: farm worker   55 **holler some** (AE infml): make some noise

having remorses every time an evangelist comes to town. No, ma'am, I'd say likker ain't a regular thing in the home here, except in the medicine chest. Right good for snake bite, y'know – always was.

BELLIGERENT MAN AT BACK OF AUDITORIUM: Is there no one in town aware of –   5

STAGE MANAGER: Come forward, will you, where we can all hear you – What were you saying?

BELLIGERENT MAN: Is there no one in town aware of social injustice and industrial inequality?

MR. WEBB: Oh, yes, everybody is – somethin' terrible. Seems like they   10 spend most of their time talking about who's rich and who's poor.

BELLIGERENT MAN: Then why don't they do something about it?

He withdraws without waiting for an answer.

MR. WEBB: Well, I dunno. … I guess we're all hunting like everybody else for a way the diligent and sensible can rise to the top and the   15 lazy and quarrelsome can sink to the bottom. But it ain't easy to find. Meanwhile, we do all we can to help those that can't help themselves and those that can we leave alone. – Are there any other questions?

LADY IN A BOX: Oh, Mr. Webb? Mr. Webb, is there any culture or love of beauty in Grover's Corners?   20

MR. WEBB: Well, ma'am, there ain't much – not in the sense you mean. Come to think of it, there's some girls that play the piano at High School Commencement; but they ain't happy about it. No, ma'am, there isn't much culture; but maybe this is the place to tell you that we've got a lot of pleasures of a kind here: we like the sun comin' up   25 over the mountain in the morning, and we all notice a good deal about the birds. We pay a lot of attention to them. And we watch the change of the seasons; yes, everybody knows about them. But those other things – you're right, ma'am, – there ain't much. – *Robinson Crusoe* and the Bible; and Handel's "Largo," we all know that; and   30 Whistler's "Mother" – those are just about as far as we go.

LADY IN A BOX: So I thought. Thank you, Mr. Webb.

STAGE MANAGER: Thank you, Mr. Webb.

MR. WEBB *retires.*

35 Now, we'll go back to the town. It's early afternoon. All 2,642 have had their dinners and all the dishes have been washed.

MR. WEBB, *having removed his coat, returns and starts pushing a lawn mover to and fro beside his house.*

There's an early-afternoon calm in our town: a buzzin' and a hummin'
40 from the school buildings; only a few buggies on Main Street – the horses dozing at the hitching posts; you all remember what it's like. Doc Gibbs is in his office, tapping people and making them say "ah." Mr. Webb's cuttin' his lawn over there; one man in ten thinks it's a privilege to push his own lawn mower.

45 No, sir. It's later than I thought. There are the children coming home from school already.

Shrill girls' voices are heard, off left. EMILY *comes along Main Street, carrying some books. There are some signs that she is imagining herself to be a lady of startling elegance.*

50 **EMILY:** *I can't,* Lois. I've got to go home and help my mother. I promised.

MR. WEBB: Emily, walk simply. Who do you think you are today?

EMILY: Papa, you're terrible. One minute you tell me to stand up straight and the next minute you call me names. I just don't listen to you.

55 *She gives him an abrupt kiss.*

MR. WEBB: Golly, I never got a kiss from such a great lady before.

He goes out of sight. EMILY *leans over and picks some flowers by the gate of her house.*

---

1 **have remorses** (non-standard): feel sorry about sth.   2 **likker** (non-standard pron) = **liquor** (AE): alcohol   4 **belligerent**: aggressive, angry   9 **inequality**: Ungleichheit   14 **I dunno** (non-standard pron): I don't know   15 **diligent**: hardworking   16 **quarrelsome**: streitlustig   22–23 **High School Commencement** (AE): ceremony at which awards are given to students   34 **retire**: (here) exit   37 **lawn mower**: Rasenmäher   38 **to and fro**: hin und her   40 **buggy**: small horsedrawn carriage   42 **tap sb.**: jdn. abklopfen   55 **abrupt**: quick and unexpected

GEORGE GIBBS *comes careening down Main Street. He is throwing a ball up to dizzying heights, and waiting to catch it again. This sometimes requires his taking six steps backward. He bumps into an Old Lady invisible to us.*

GEORGE: Excuse me, Mrs. Forrest.

STAGE MANAGER: *[As Mrs. Forrest.]* Go out and play in the fields, young   5
man. You got no business playing baseball on Main Street.

GEORGE: Awfully sorry, Mrs. Forrest. – Hello, Emily.

EMILY: H'lo.

GEORGE: You made a fine speech in class.

EMILY: Well … I was really ready to make a speech about the Monroe   10
Doctrine, but at the last minute Miss Corcoran made me talk about
the Louisiana Purchase instead. I worked an awful long time on both
of them.

GEORGE: Gee, it's funny, Emily. From my window up there I can just see
your head nights when you're doing your homework over in your   15
room.

EMILY: Why, can you?

GEORGE: You certainly do stick to it, Emily. I don't see how you can sit
still that long. I guess you like school.

EMILY: Well, I always feel it's something you have to go through.   20

GEORGE: Yeah.

EMILY: I don't mind it really. It passes the time.

GEORGE: Yeah. – Emily, what do you think? We might work out a kinda
telegraph from your window to mine; and once in a while you could
give me a kinda hint or two about one of those algebra problems. I   25
don't mean the answers, Emily, of course not … just some little
hint …

EMILY: Oh, I think *hints* are allowed. – So – ah – if you get stuck, George,
you whistle to me; and I'll give you some hints.

GEORGE: Emily, you're just naturally bright, I guess.   30

EMILY: I figure that it's just the way a person's born.

GEORGE: Yeah. But, you see, I want to be a farmer, and my Uncle Luke says whenever I'm ready I can come over and work on his farm and if I'm any good I can just gradually have it.

35 **EMILY:** You mean the house and everything?

Enter MRS. WEBB *with a large bowl and sits on the bench by her trellis.*

GEORGE: Yeah. Well, thanks ... I better be getting out to the baseball field. Thanks for the talk, Emily. – Good afternoon, Mrs. Webb.

MRS. WEBB: Good afternoon, George.

40 **GEORGE:** So long, Emily.

EMILY: So long, George.

MRS. WEBB: Emily, come and help me string these beans for the winter. George Gibbs let himself have a real conversation, didn't he? Why, he's growing up. How old would George be?

45 **EMILY:** I don't know.

MRS. WEBB: Let's see. He must be almost sixteen.

EMILY: Mama, I made a speech in class today and I was very good.

MRS. WEBB: You must recite it to your father at supper. What was it about?

50 **EMILY:** The Louisiana Purchase. It was like silk off a spool. I'm going to make speeches all my life. – Mama, are these big enough?

MRS. WEBB: Try and get them a little bigger if you can.

EMILY: Mama, will you answer me a question, serious?

MRS. WEBB: Seriously, dear – not serious.

---

1 **careen**: run fast   2 **dizzying**: Schwindel erregend   8 **h'lo** (non-standard pron): hello   10–11 **Monroe Doctrine**: principle of US foreign policy (formulated in 1823) that opposes the influence of outside powers in the affairs of the American continent   12 **the Louisiana Purchase**: the buying of land west of the Mississippi River from France in 1803   18 **stick to sth.**: keep on doing sth.   48 **recite sth.**: etwas vortragen   50 **it was like silk off a spool**: it went very easily (**silk**: Seide; **spool**: Rolle)

EMILY: Seriously, – will you?

MRS. WEBB: Of course, I will.

EMILY: Mama, am I good looking?

MRS. WEBB: Yes, of course you are. All my children have got good features; I'd be ashamed if they hadn't.   5

EMILY: Oh, Mama, that's not what I mean. What I mean is: am I *pretty*?

MRS. WEBB: I've already told you, yes. Now that's enough of that. You have a nice young pretty face. I never heard of such foolishness.

EMILY: Oh, Mama, you never tell us the truth about anything.

MRS. WEBB: I *am* telling you the truth.   10

EMILY: Mama, were *you* pretty?

MRS. WEBB: Yes, I was, if I do say it. I was the prettiest girl in town next to Mamie Cartwright.

EMILY: But, Mama, you've got to say *some*thing about me. Am I pretty enough … to get anybody … to get people interested in me?   15

MRS. WEBB: Emily, you make me tired. Now stop it. You're pretty enough for all normal purposes. – Come along now and bring that bowl with you.

EMILY: Oh, Mama, you're no help at all.

STAGE MANAGER: Thank you. Thank you! That'll do. We'll have to   20 interrupt again here. Thank you, Mrs. Webb; thank you, Emily.

MRS. WEBB *and* EMILY *withdraw.*

There are some more things we want to explore about this town.

He comes to the center of the stage. During the following speech the lights gradually dim to darkness, leaving only a spot on him.   25

I think this is a good time to tell you that the Cartwright interests have just begun building a new bank in Grover's Corners – had to go to Vermont for the marble, sorry to say. And they've asked a friend of mine what they should put in the cornerstone for people to dig up … a thousand years from now. … Of course, they've put in a copy of   30 the *New York Times* and a copy of Mr. Webb's *Sentinel*. … We're kind of interested in this because some scientific fellas have found a way of painting all that reading matter with a glue – a silicate glue – that'll make it keep a thousand – two thousand years.

35 We're putting in a Bible … and the Constitution of the United States – and a copy of William Shakespeare's plays. What do you say, folks? What do you think?

Y'know – Babylon once had two million people in it, and all we know about 'em is the names of the kings and some copies of wheat
40 contracts … and contracts for the sale of slaves. Yet every night all those families sat down to supper, and the father came home from his work, and the smoke went up the chimney, – same as here. And even in Greece and Rome, all we know about the *real* life of the people is what we can piece together out of the joking poems and the
45 comedies they wrote for the theatre back then.

So I'm going to have a copy of this play put in the cornerstone and the people a thousand years from now'll know a few simple facts about us – more than the Treaty of Versailles and the Lindbergh flight.

50 See what I mean?

So – people a thousand years from now – this is the way we were in the provinces north of New York at the beginning of the twentieth century. – This is the way we were: in our growing up and in our marrying and in our living and in our dying.

55 *A choir partially concealed in the orchestra pit has begun singing "Blessed Be the Tie That Binds."*

4–5 **have good features**: be good-looking   12–13 **next to**: except for   25 **dim** (v): become darker   **spot**: spotlight   26 **the Cartwright interests**: the people in control of the Cartwright family fortune   28 **marble**: Marmor   29 **cornerstone**: Grundstein   33 **silicate glue**: Klebstoff auf Siliziumbasis   39 **wheat**: Weizen   42 **chimney**: Kamin   48 **Treaty of Versailles, the Lindbergh flight**: examples of famous world events of the time (the former concluding the First World War, the latter being the first non-stop flight across the Atlantic Ocean by Charles Lindbergh in 1927)   52 **provinces**: (here) area beyond major cities and town   55 **"Blessed Be …"**: Kirchenlied

SIMON STIMSON *stands directing them.*

Two ladders have been pushed onto the stage; they serve as indication of the second story in the Gibbs and Webb houses. GEORGE *and* EMILY *mount them, and apply themselves to their schoolwork.*

DR. GIBBS *has entered and is seated in his kitchen reading.*   5

Well! – good deal of time's gone by. It's evening.

You can hear choir practice going on in the Congregational Church.

The children are at home doing their schoolwork.

The day's running down like a tired clock.

SIMON STIMSON: Now look here, everybody. Music come into the   10
world to give pleasure. – Softer! Softer! Get it out of your heads that
music's only good when it's loud. You leave loudness to the
Methodists. You couldn't beat 'em, even if you wanted to. Now again.
Tenors!

GEORGE: Hssst! Emily!   15

EMILY: Hello.

GEORGE: Hello!

EMILY: I can't work at all. The moonlight's so *terrible*.

GEORGE: Emily, did you get the third problem?

EMILY: Which?   20

GEORGE: The *third*?

EMILY: Why, yes, George – that's the easiest of them all.

GEORGE: I don't see it. Emily, can you give me a hint?

EMILY: I'll tell you one thing: the answer's in yards.

GEORGE: !!! In yards? How do you mean?   25

EMILY: In *square* yards.

GEORGE: Oh … in square yards.

EMILY: Yes, George, don't you see?

GEORGE: Yeah.

30 **EMILY:** In square yards of *wallpaper*.

GEORGE: Wallpaper, – oh, I see. Thanks a lot, Emily.

EMILY: You're welcome. My, isn't the moonlight *terrible*? And choir practice going on. – I think if you hold your breath you can hear the train all the way to Contoocook. Hear it?

35 **GEORGE:** M-m-m – What do you know!

EMILY: Well, I guess I better go back and try to work.

GEORGE: Good night, Emily. And thanks.

EMILY: Good night, George.

SIMON STIMSON: Before I forget it: how many of you will be able to
40 come in Tuesday afternoon and sing at Fred Hersey's wedding? – show your hands. That'll be fine; that'll be right nice. We'll do the same music we did for Jane Trowbridge's last month.

– Now we'll do "Art Thou Weary; Art Thou Languid?" It's a question, ladies and gentlemen, make it talk. Ready.

45 **DR. GIBBS:** Oh, George, can you come down a minute?

GEORGE: Yes, Pa.

He descends the ladder.

DR. GIBBS: Make yourself comfortable, George; I'll only keep you a minute. George, how old are you?

50 **GEORGE:** I? I'm sixteen, almost seventeen.

DR. GIBBS: What do you want to do after school's over?

GEORGE: Why, you know, Pa. I want to be a farmer on Uncle Luke's farm.

---

2 **ladder**: Leiter　**serve as indication of sth.**: auf etwas deuten　3 **mount sth.**: climb sth.　4 **apply yourself to sth.**: concentrate on doing sth.　9 **run down**: auslaufen　24 **yard**: Maßeinheit (ca. 91,44 cm)　26 **square yard**: Yard im Quadrat　30 **wallpaper**: Tapete　41 **right nice** (AE): very nice　43 "**Art Thou Weary …**": Kirchenlied　47 **descend sth.**: go down sth.

DR. GIBBS: You'll be willing, will you, to get up early and milk and feed the stock … and you'll be able to hoe and hay all day?

GEORGE: Sure, I will. What are you … what do you mean, Pa?

DR. GIBBS: Well, George, while I was in my office today I heard a funny sound … and what do you think it was? It was your mother chopping 5
wood. There you see your mother – getting up early; cooking meals all day long; washing and ironing; – and still she has to go out in the back yard and chop wood. I suppose she just got tired of asking you. She just gave up and decided it was easier to do it herself. And you eat her meals, and put on the clothes she keeps nice for you, and you 10
run off and play baseball, – like she's some hired girl we keep around the house but that we don't like very much. Well, I knew all I had to do was call your attention to it. Here's a handkerchief, son. George, I've decided to raise your spending money twenty-five cents a week. Not, of course, for chopping wood for your mother, because that's a 15
present you give her, but because you're getting older – and I imagine there are lots of things you must find to do with it.

GEORGE: Thanks, Pa.

DR. GIBBS: Let's see – tomorrow's your payday. You can count on it – Hmm. Probably Rebecca'll feel she ought to have some more too. 20
Wonder what could have happened to your mother. Choir practice never was as late as this before.

GEORGE: It's only half past eight, Pa.

DR. GIBBS: I don't know why she's in that old choir. She hasn't any more voice than an old crow. … Traipsin' around the streets at this hour of 25
the night … Just about time you retired, don't you think?

GEORGE: Yes, Pa.

GEORGE *mounts to his place on the ladder.*

Laughter and good nights can be heard on stage left and presently MRS. GIBBS,
MRS. SOAMES *and* MRS. WEBB *come down Main Street. When they arrive at the* 30
corner of the stage they stop.

MRS. SOAMES: Good night, Martha. Good night, Mr. Foster.

MRS. WEBB: I'll tell Mr. Webb; I *know* he'll want to put it in the paper.

MRS. GIBBS: My, it's late!

35 **MRS. SOAMES:** Good night, Irma.

MRS. GIBBS: Real nice choir practice, wa'n't it? Myrtle Webb! Look at that moon, will you! Tsk-tsk-tsk. Potato weather, for sure.

They are silent a moment, gazing up at the moon.

MRS. SOAMES: Naturally I didn't want to say a word about it in front of
40 those others, but now we're alone – really, it's the worst scandal that ever was in this town!

MRS. GIBBS: What?

MRS. SOAMES: Simon Stimson!

MRS. GIBBS: Now, Louella!

45 **MRS. SOAMES:** But, Julia! To have the organist of a church *drink* and *drunk* year after year. You know he was drunk tonight.

MRS. GIBBS: Now, Louella! We all know about Mr. Stimson, and we all know about the troubles he's been through, and Dr. Ferguson knows too, and if Dr. Ferguson keeps him on there in his job the only thing
50 the rest of us can do is just not to notice it.

MRS. SOAMES: *Not to notice it!* But it's getting worse.

MRS. WEBB: No, it isn't, Louella. It's getting better. I've been in that choir twice as long as you have. It doesn't happen anywhere near so often. … My, I hate to go to bed on a night like this. – I better hurry. Those
55 children'll be sitting up till all hours. Good night, Louella.

They all exchange good nights. She hurries downstage, enters her house and disappears.

MRS. GIBBS: Can you get home safe, Louella?

---

2 **stock**: animals on a farm   **hoe and hay**: work with a hoe (= Hacke) and feed
the animals hay (= Heu)   5 **chop sth.**: etwas hacken   7 **iron** (v): bügeln
11 **hired girl**: paid servant   19 **payday**: day on which a worker receives his or her
money   25 **crow**: Krähe   26 **retire**: (here) go to bed   36 **wa'n't it** (non-standard
pron): wasn't it   37 **potato weather** (AE): warm and dry weather   55 **till all
hours**: (here) very late

MRS. SOAMES: It's as bright as day. I can see Mr. Soames scowling at the window now. You'd think we'd been to a dance the way the men-folk carry on.

More good nights. MRS. GIBBS *arrives at her home and passes through the trellis into the kitchen.*   5

MRS. GIBBS: Well, we had a real good time.

DR. GIBBS: You're late enough.

MRS. GIBBS: Why, Frank, it ain't any later 'n usual.

DR. GIBBS: And you stopping at the corner to gossip with a lot of hens.

MRS. GIBBS: Now, Frank, don't be grouchy. Come out and smell the   10
heliotrope in the moonlight.

They stroll out arm in arm along the footlights.

Isn't that wonderful? What did you do all the time I was away?

DR. GIBBS: Oh, I read – as usual. What were the girls gossiping about tonight?   15

MRS. GIBBS: Well, believe me, Frank – there is something to gossip about.

DR. GIBBS: Hmm! Simon Stimson far gone, was he?

MRS. GIBBS: Worst I ever seen him. How'll that end, Frank? Dr. Ferguson can't forgive him forever.   20

DR. GIBBS: I guess I know more about Simon Stimson's affairs than anybody in this town. Some people ain't made for small-town life. I don't know how that'll end; but there's nothing we can do but just leave it alone. Come, get in.

MRS. GIBBS: No, not yet … Frank, I'm worried about you.   25

DR. GIBBS: What are you worried about?

MRS. GIBBS: I think it's my duty to make plans for you to get a real rest and change. And if I get that legacy, well, I'm going to insist on it.

DR. GIBBS: Now, Julia, there's no sense in going over that again.

MRS. GIBBS: Frank, you're just *unreasonable*!   30

DR. GIBBS: *[Starting into the house.]* Come on, Julia, it's getting late. First thing you know you'll catch cold. I gave George a piece of my mind tonight. I reckon you'll have your wood chopped for a while anyway. No, no, start getting upstairs.

35 MRS. GIBBS: Oh, dear. There's always so many things to pick up, seems like. You know, Frank, Mrs. Fairchild always locks her front door every night. All those people up that part of town do.

DR. GIBBS: *[Blowing out the lamp.]* They're all getting citified, that's the trouble with them. They haven't got nothing fit to burgle and 40 everybody knows it.

They disappear.

REBECCA *climbs up the ladder beside* GEORGE.

GEORGE: Get out, Rebecca. There's only room for one at this window. You're always spoiling everything.

45 REBECCA: Well, let me look just a minute.

GEORGE: Use your own window.

REBECCA: I did, but there's no moon there. … George, do you know what I think, do you? I think maybe the moon's getting nearer and nearer and there'll be a big 'splosion.

50 GEORGE: Rebecca, you don't know anything. If the moon were getting nearer, the guys that sit up all night with telescopes would see it first and they'd tell about it, and it'd be in all the newspapers.

---

1 **scowl**: grimmig blicken   7 **it ain't any later'n usual** (non-standard): it isn't later than usual   9 **gossip**: tratschen   10 **grouchy**: bad-tempered   11 **heliotrope**: type of flower   12 **stroll**: walk slowly and easily   18 **far gone**: (here) drunk 19 **worst I ever seen him** (non-standard): the worst state I have ever seen him in   21 **affairs** (pl): life, business   28 **insist on sth.**: auf etwas bestehen 31–32 **first thing you know**: before you realize it   32 **give sb. a piece of your mind**: tell sb. exactly what you think about sb./sth.   38 **citified**: (here) adapted to the needs of urban life rather than country living   39 **nothing fit to burgle**: nothing worth stealing   44 **spoil sth.**: ruin sth., make sth. less good   49 **'splosion** (non-standard pron): explosion

REBECCA: George, is the moon shining on South America, Canada and half the whole world?

GEORGE: Well – prob'ly is.

The STAGE MANAGER *strolls on.*

Pause. The sound of crickets is heard.   5

STAGE MANAGER: Nine thirty. Most of the lights are out. No, there's Constable Warren trying a few doors on Main Street. And here comes Editor Webb, after putting his newspaper to bed.

Mr. Warren, an elderly policeman, comes along Main Street from the right, MR. WEBB *from the left.*   10

MR. WEBB: Good evening, Bill.

CONSTABLE WARREN: Evenin', Mr. Webb.

MR. WEBB: Quite a moon!

CONSTABLE WARREN: Yepp.

MR. WEBB: All quiet tonight?   15

CONSTABLE WARREN: Simon Stimson is rollin' around a little. Just saw his wife movin' out to hunt for him so I looked the other way – there he is now.

SIMON STIMSON *comes down Main Street from the left, only a trace of unsteadiness in his walk.*   20

MR. WEBB: Good evening, Simon … Town seems to have settled down for the night pretty well. …

SIMON STIMSON *comes up to him and pauses a moment and stares at him, swaying slightly.*

Good evening … Yes, most of the town's settled down for the night,   25
Simon. … I guess we better do the same. Can I walk along a ways
with you?

SIMON STIMSON *continues on his way without a word and disappears at the right.*

Good night.   30

CONSTABLE WARREN: I don't know how that's goin' to end, Mr. Webb.

MR. WEBB: Well, he's seen a peck of trouble, one thing after another. … Oh, Bill … if you see my boy smoking cigarettes, just give him a word, will you? He thinks a lot of you, Bill.

35   **CONSTABLE WARREN:** I don't think he smokes no cigarettes, Mr. Webb. Leastways, not more'n two or three a year.

MR. WEBB: Hm … I hope not. – Well, good night, Bill.

CONSTABLE WARREN: Good night, Mr. Webb.

Exit.

40   **MR. WEBB:** Who's that up there? Is that you, Myrtle?

EMILY: No, it's me, Papa.

MR. WEBB: Why aren't you in bed?

EMILY: I don't know. I just can't sleep yet, Papa. The moonlight's so wonderful. And the smell of Mrs. Gibbs' heliotrope. Can you smell it?

45   **MR. WEBB:** Hm … Yes. Haven't any troubles on your mind, have you, Emily?

EMILY: Troubles, Papa? No.

MR. WEBB: Well, enjoy yourself, but don't let your mother catch you. Good night, Emily.

50   **EMILY:** Good night, Papa.

MR. WEBB *crosses into the house, whistling "Blessed Be the Tie That Binds" and disappears.*

REBECCA: I never told you about that letter Jane Crofut got from her minister when she was sick. He wrote Jane a letter and on the
55   envelope the address was like this: It said: Jane Crofut; The Crofut Farm; Grover's Corners; Sutton County; New Hampshire; United States of America.

---

5 **cricket**: Grille   16 **roll around** (AE): stagger around, walk unsteadily
19–20 **a trace of unsteadiness in his walk**: (here) having difficulty walking
24 **sway**: schwanken   26–27 **walk along a ways with sb.**: (here) walk along
together with sb.   32 **a peck of trouble** (AE): a lot of trouble   36 **leastways** (AE):
at least

GEORGE: What's funny about that?

REBECCA: But listen, it's not finished: the United States of America; Continent of North America; Western Hemisphere; the Earth; the Solar System; the Universe; the Mind of God – that's what it said on the envelope.   5

GEORGE: What do you know!

REBECCA: And the postman brought it just the same.

GEORGE: What do you know!

STAGE MANAGER: That's the end of the First Act, friends. You can go and smoke now, those that smoke.   10

Act II

The tables and chairs of the two kitchens are still on the stage. The ladders and the small bench have been withdrawn. The STAGE MANAGER *has been at his accustomed place watching the audience return to its seats.*

STAGE MANAGER: Three years have gone by.

15   Yes, the sun's come up over a thousand times.

Summers and winters have cracked the mountains a little bit more and the rains have brought down some of the dirt.

Some babies that weren't even born before have begun talking regular sentences already; and a number of people who thought they were
20   right young and spry have noticed that they can't bound up a flight of stairs like they used to, without their heart fluttering a little.

All that can happen in a thousand days.

Nature's been pushing and contriving in other ways, too: a number of young people fell in love and got married.

25   Yes, the mountain got bit away a few fractions of an inch; millions of gallons of water went by the mill; and here and there a new home was set up under a roof.

Almost everybody in the world gets married, – you know what I mean? In our town there aren't hardly any exceptions. Most
30   everybody in the world climbs into their graves married.

The First Act was called the Daily Life. This act is called Love and Marriage. There's another act coming after this: I reckon you can guess what that's about.

---

4 **the Solar System**: Sonnensystem   13 **accustomed**: (here) usual   20 **right young** (AE): still young   **spry**: fit, active   **bound up sth.**: run up sth.   21 **flutter**: flattern   23 **contrive**: arrange (sth.), make plans   25 **bit** (non-standard): bitten (past participle of "bite")   26 **mill**: Mühle   29 **most** (non-standard pron): almost

So:

It's three years later. It's 1904.

It's July 7th, just after High School Commencement.

That's the time most of our young people jump up and get married.

Soon as they've passed their last examinations in solid geometry and   5
Cicero's Orations, looks like they suddenly feel themselves fit to be
married.

It's early morning. Only this time it's been raining. It's been pouring
and thundering.

Mrs. Gibbs' garden, and Mrs. Webb's here: drenched.   10

All those bean poles and pea vines: drenched.

All yesterday over there on Main Street, the rain looked like curtains
being blown along.

Hm … it may begin again any minute.

There! You can hear 5:45 for Boston.   15

MRS. GIBBS *and* MRS. WEBB *enter their kitchens and start the day as in the First
Act.*

And there's Mrs. Gibbs and Mrs. Webb come down to make breakfast,
just as though it were an ordinary day. I don't have to point out to the
women in my audience that those ladies they see before them, both   20
of those ladies cooked three meals a day – one of 'em for twenty
years, the other for forty – and no summer vacation. They brought
up two children apiece, washed, cleaned the house, – and *never a
nervous breakdown.*

It's like what one of those Middle West poets said: You've got to love   25
life to have life, and you've got to have life to love life. … It's what
they call a vicious circle.

HOWIE NEWSOME: *[Off stage left.]* Giddap, Bessie!

STAGE MANAGER: Here comes Howie Newsome delivering the milk.
And there's Si Crowell delivering the papers like his brother before   30
him.

SI CROWELL *has entered hurling imaginary newspapers into doorways;* HOWIE NEWSOME *has come along Main Street with Bessie.*

SI CROWELL: Morning, Howie.

35 **HOWIE NEWSOME:** Morning, Si. – Anything in the papers I ought to know?

SI CROWELL: Nothing much, except we're losing about the best baseball pitcher Grover's Corners ever had – George Gibbs.

HOWIE NEWSOME: Reckon he is.

40 **SI CROWELL:** He could hit and run bases, too.

HOWIE NEWSOME: Yep. Mighty fine ball player. – Whoa! Bessie! I guess I can stop and talk if I've a mind to!

SI CROWELL: I don't see how he could give up a thing like that just to get married. Would you, Howie?

45 **HOWIE NEWSOME:** Can't tell, Si. Never had no talent that way.

CONSTABLE WARREN *enters. They exchange good mornings.*

You're up early, Bill.

CONSTABLE WARREN: Seein' if there's anything I can do to prevent a flood. River's been risin' all night.

50 **HOWIE NEWSOME:** Si Crowell's all worked up here about George Gibbs' retiring from baseball.

CONSTABLE WARREN: Yes, sir; that's the way it goes. Back in '84 we had a player, Si – even George Gibbs couldn't touch him. Name of Hank Todd. Went down to Maine and become a parson. Wonderful ball
55   player. – Howie, how does the weather look to you?

---

5 **solid geometry**: study of geometric forms   6 **Cicero's Orations**: Latin texts by Cicero   8 **pour**: rain heavily   10 **drenched**: very wet   11 **bean pole**: Bohnenstange   23 **apiece**: each   24 **nervous breakdown**: Nervenzusammenbruch   27 **vicious circle**: Teufelskreis   37–38 **baseball pitcher**: player who throws the ball   39 **reckon**: (I) think   40 **run bases**: (in baseball) run from base to base to score a "run"   41 **mighty fine** (AE): very good   42 **have a mind to do sth.**: (here) want to do sth.   48 **prevent sth.**: stop sth. from happening   49 **rise**: (of a river level) get higher   54 **parson**: Protestant minister or preacher

HOWIE NEWSOME: Oh, 'tain't bad. Think maybe it'll clear up for good.

CONSTABLE WARREN *and* SI CROWELL *continue on their way.*

HOWIE NEWSOME *brings the milk first to Mrs. Gibbs' house. She meets him by the trellis.*

MRS. GIBBS: Good morning, Howie. Do you think it's going to rain again?   5

HOWIE NEWSOME: Morning, Mrs. Gibbs. It rained so heavy, I think maybe it'll clear up.

MRS. GIBBS: Certainly hope it will.

HOWIE NEWSOME: How much did you want today?   10

MRS. GIBBS: I'm going to have a houseful of relations, Howie. Looks to me like I'll need three-a-milk and two-a-cream.

HOWIE NEWSOME: My wife says to tell you we both hope they'll be very happy, Mrs. Gibbs. Know they *will*.

MRS. GIBBS: Thanks a lot, Howie. Tell your wife I hope she gits there to the wedding.   15

HOWIE NEWSOME: Yes, she'll be there; she'll be there if she kin.

HOWIE NEWSOME *crosses to Mrs. Webb's house.*

Morning, Mrs. Webb.

MRS. WEBB: Oh, good morning, Mr. Newsome. I told you four quarts of milk, but I hope you can spare me another.   20

HOWIE NEWSOME: Yes'm ... and the two of cream.

MRS. WEBB: Will it start raining again, Mr. Newsome?

HOWIE NEWSOME: Well. Just sayin' to Mrs. Gibbs as how it may lighten up. Mrs. Newsome told me to tell you as how we hope they'll both be very happy, Mrs. Webb. Know they *will*.   25

MRS. WEBB: Thank you, and thank Mrs. Newsome and we're counting on seeing you at the wedding.

HOWIE NEWSOME: Yes, Mrs. Webb. We hope to git there. Couldn't miss that. Come on, Bessie.   30

Exit HOWIE NEWSOME.

DR. GIBBS *descends in shirt sleeves, and sits down at his breakfast table.*

DR. GIBBS: Well, Ma, the day has come. You're losin' one of your chicks.

35 **MRS. GIBBS:** Frank Gibbs, don't you say another word. I feel like crying every minute. Sit down and drink your coffee.

DR. GIBBS: The groom's up shaving himself – only there ain't an awful lot to shave. Whistling and singing, like he's glad to leave us. – Every now and then he says "I do" to the mirror, but it don't sound
40 convincing to me.

MRS. GIBBS: I declare, Frank, I don't know how he'll get along. I've arranged his clothes and seen to it he's put warm things on, – Frank! they're too *young*. Emily won't think of such things. He'll catch his death of cold within a week.

45 **DR. GIBBS:** I was remembering my wedding morning, Julia.

MRS. GIBBS: Now don't start that, Frank Gibbs.

DR. GIBBS: I was the scaredest young fella in the State of New Hampshire. I thought I'd make a mistake for sure. And when I saw you comin' down that aisle I thought you were the prettiest girl I'd ever seen, but
50 the only trouble was that I'd never seen you before. There I was in the Congregational Church marryin' a total stranger.

MRS. GIBBS: And how do you think I felt! – Frank, weddings are perfectly awful things. Farces, – that's what they are!

She puts a plate before him.

55 Here, I've made something for you.

DR. GIBBS: Why, Julia Hersey – French toast!

---

12 **three-a-milk and two-a-cream**: three bottles of milk and two of cream   15 **gits** (non-standard pron): gets   17 **kin** (non-standard pron): can   22 **'m = ma'am**: madam   24–25 **lighten up**: (of weather) improve   27 **count on sth.**: expect sth.   34 **chick**: (here) children   37 **groom**: Bräutigam   40 **convincing** (adj): überzeugend   47 **the scaredest** (non-standard): the most scared   53 **farce**: ridiculous event   56 **French toast**: toast fried with egg and milk

MRS. GIBBS: 'Tain't hard to make and I had to do *something*.

Pause. DR. GIBBS *pours on the syrup.*

DR. GIBBS: How'd you sleep last night, Julia?

MRS. GIBBS: Well, I heard a lot of the hours struck off.

DR. GIBBS: Ye-e-s! I get a shock every time I think of George setting out   5
to be a family man – that great gangling thing! – I tell you Julia,
there's nothing so terrifying in the world as a *son*. The relation of
father and son is the darndest, awkwardest –

MRS. GIBBS: Well, mother and daughter's no picnic, let me tell you.

DR. GIBBS: They'll have a lot of troubles, I suppose, but that's none of   10
our business. Everybody has a right to their own troubles.

MRS. GIBBS: *[At the table, drinking her coffee, meditatively.]* Yes … people
are meant to go through life two by two. 'Tain't natural to be
lonesome.

Pause. DR. GIBBS *starts laughing.*   15

DR. GIBBS: Julia, do you know one of the things I was scared of when I
married you?

MRS. GIBBS: Oh, go along with you!

DR. GIBBS: I was afraid we wouldn't have material for conversation
more'n'd last us a few weeks.   20

Both laugh.

I was afraid we'd run out and eat our meals in silence, that's a fact. –
Well, you and I been conversing for twenty years now without any
noticeable barren spells.

MRS. GIBBS: Well, – good weather, bad weather – 'tain't very choice, but   25
I always find something to say.

She goes to the foot of the stairs.

Did you hear Rebecca stirring around upstairs?

DR. GIBBS: No. Only day of the year Rebecca hasn't been managing
everybody's business up there. She's hiding in her room. – I got the   30
impression she's crying.

MRS. GIBBS: Lord's sakes! – This has got to stop. – Rebecca! Rebecca! Come and get your breakfast.

GEORGE *comes rattling down the stairs, very brisk.*

35 **GEORGE:** Good morning, everybody. Only five more hours to live.

Makes the gesture of cutting his throat, and a loud "k-k-k," and starts through the trellis.

MRS. GIBBS: George Gibbs, where are you going?

GEORGE: Just stepping across the grass to see my girl.

40 **MRS. GIBBS:** Now, George! You put on your overshoes. It's raining torrents. You don't go out of this house without you're prepared for it.

GEORGE: Aw. Ma. It's just a *step!*

MRS. GIBBS: George! You'll catch your death of cold and cough all
45 through the service.

DR. GIBBS: George, do as your mother tells you!

DR. GIBBS *goes upstairs.*

GEORGE *returns reluctantly to the kitchen and pantomimes putting on overshoes.*

50 **MRS. GIBBS:** From tomorrow on you can kill yourself in all weathers, but while you're in my house you'll live wisely, thank you. – Maybe Mrs. Webb isn't used to callers at seven in the morning. – Here, take a cup of coffee first.

---

4 **hear the hours struck off**: hear a clock striking the hours   6 **gangling**: tall and thin with long arms and legs   8 **darndest** (AE): strangest   **awkwardest** (non-standard): most awkward   9 **sth. is no picnic**: sth. is not easy   12 **meditatively**: thoughtfully   14 **lonesome** (AE): lonely   19 **material for conversation**: things to talk about   20 **more'n'd** (non-standard): more than would   24 **barren spells**: times when nothing happens   25 **'tain't very choice** (AE, non-standard): it isn't always the best   28 **stir**: move around   32 **Lord's sakes!**: Um Gottes willen!   34 **rattle**: klappern   41 **torrent**: strong rainfall   **without** (non-standard): (here) unless   44 **service**: church ceremony; (here) wedding   48 **reluctantly**: not really wanting to do sth.   **pantomime sth.**: act out sth.

GEORGE: Be back in a minute.

He crosses the stage, leaping over the puddles.

Good morning, Mother Webb.

MRS. WEBB: Goodness! You frightened me! – Now, George, you can
come in a minute out of the wet, but you know I can't ask you in.   5

GEORGE: Why not –?

MRS. WEBB: George, you know's well as I do: the groom can't see his
bride on his wedding day, not until he sees her in church.

GEORGE: Aw! – that's just a superstition. – Good morning, Mr. Webb.

Enter MR. WEBB.   10

MR. WEBB: Good morning, George.

GEORGE: Mr. Webb, you don't believe in that superstition, do you?

MR. WEBB: There's a lot of common sense in some superstitions,
George.

He sits at the table, facing right.   15

MRS. WEBB: Millions have folla'd it, George, and you don't want to be
the first to fly in the face of custom.

GEORGE: How is Emily?

MRS. WEBB: She hasn't waked up yet. I haven't heard a sound out of
her.   20

GEORGE: Emily's *asleep!!!*

MRS. WEBB: No wonder! We were up 'til all hours, sewing and packing.
Now I'll tell you what I'll do; you set down here a minute with Mr.
Webb and drink this cup of coffee; and I'll go upstairs and see she
doesn't come down and surprise you. There's some bacon, too; but   25
don't be long about it.

Exit MRS. WEBB.

Embarrassed silence.

MR. WEBB *dunks doughnuts in his coffee.*

More silence.   30

MR. WEBB: *[Suddenly and loudly.]* Well, George, how are you?

GEORGE: *[Startled, choking over his coffee.]* Oh, fine, I'm fine.

Pause.

Mr. Webb, what sense could there be in a superstition like that?

35   **MR. WEBB:** Well, you see, – on her wedding morning a girl's head's apt to be full of ... clothes and one thing and another. Don't you think that's probably it?

GEORGE: Ye-e-s. I never thought of that.

MR. WEBB: A girl's apt to be a mite nervous on her wedding day.

40   *Pause.*

GEORGE: I wish a fellow could get married without all that marching up and down.

MR. WEBB: Every man that's ever lived has felt that way about it, George; but it hasn't been any use. It's the womenfolk who've built up 45   weddings, my boy. For a while now the women have it all their own. A man looks pretty small at a wedding, George. All those good women standing shoulder to shoulder making sure that the knot's tied in a mighty public way.

GEORGE: But ... you *believe* in it, don't you, Mr. Webb?

50   **MR. WEBB:** *[With alacrity.]* Oh, yes; *oh, yes.* Don't you misunderstand me, my boy. Marriage is a wonderful thing, – wonderful thing. And don't you forget that, George.

GEORGE: No, sir, – Mr. Webb, how old were you when you got married?

---

2 **leap**: jump   **puddle**: small pool of rainwater   9 **superstition**: Aberglaube
16 **folla'd** (non-standard pron): followed   17 **fly in the face of custom**: do sth. that goes against tradition   19 **waked** (non-standard): woken   22 **sew**: nähen
29 **dunk sth.**: dip sth. in liquid   32 **choke over sth.**: sich an etwas verschlucken
35 **apt**: likely   39 **mite**: a little bit   47–48 **tie the knot**: get married   50 **with alacrity**: with haste, quickly

MR. WEBB: Well, you see: I'd been to college and I'd taken a little time to get settled. But Mrs. Webb – she wasn't much older than what Emily is. Oh, age hasn't much to do with it, George, – not compared with … uh … other things.

GEORGE: What were you going to say, Mr. Webb?   5

MR. WEBB: Oh, I don't know. – Was I going to say something?

Pause.

George, I was thinking the other night of some advice my father gave me when I got married. Charles, he said, Charles, start out early showing who's boss, he said. Best thing to do is to give an order, even   10
if it don't make sense; just so she'll learn to obey. And he said: if anything about your wife irritates you – her conversation, or anything – just get up and leave the house. That'll make it clear to her, he said. And, oh, yes! he said never, never let your wife know how much money you have, never.   15

GEORGE: Well, Mr. Webb … I don't think I could …

MR. WEBB: So I took the opposite of my father's advice and I've been happy ever since. And let that be a lesson to you, George, never to ask advice on personal matters. – George, are you going to raise chickens on your farm?   20

GEORGE: What?

MR. WEBB: Are you going to raise chickens on your farm?

GEORGE: Uncle Luke's never been much interested, but I thought –

MR. WEBB: A book came into my office the other day, George, on the Philo System of raising chickens. I want you to read it. I'm thinking   25
of beginning in a small way in the back yard, and I'm going to put an incubator in the cellar –

Enter MRS. WEBB.

MRS. WEBB: Charles, are you talking about that old incubator again? I thought you two'd be talking about things worth while.   30

MR. WEBB: *[Bitingly.]* Well, Myrtle, if you want to give the boy some good advice, I'll go upstairs and leave you alone with him.

MRS. WEBB: *[Pulling* GEORGE *up.]* George, Emily's got to come downstairs
and eat her breakfast. She sends you her love but she doesn't want to
35   lay eyes on you. Good-by.

GEORGE: Good-by.

GEORGE *crosses the stage to his own home, bewildered and crestfallen. He*
slowly dodges a puddle and disappears into his house.

MR. WEBB: Myrtle, I guess you don't know about that older supersti-
40   tion.

MRS. WEBB: What do you mean, Charles?

MR. WEBB: Since the cave men: no bridegroom should see his father-in-
law on the day of the wedding, or near it. Now remember that.

Both leave the stage.

45   STAGE MANAGER: Thank you very much, Mr. and Mrs. Webb. – Now I
have to interrupt again here. You see, we want to know how all this
began – this wedding, this plan to spend a lifetime together. I'm
awfully interested in how big things like that begin.

You know how it is: you're twenty-one or twenty-two and you make
50   some decisions; then whisssh! you're seventy: you've been a lawyer
for fifty rears, and that white-haired lady at your side has eaten over
fifty thousand meals with you.

How do such things begin?

George and Emily are going to show you now the conversation they
55   had when they first knew that … that … as the saying goes … they
were meant for one another.

---

10 **show sb. who's boss**: make it clear to sb. who is in control   19–20 **raise**
chickens: Hühner züchten   25 **Philo system**: system of heating through cathode-
ray tubes (= Kathodenstrahlröhre)   27 **incubator**: Brutkasten   31 **bitingly**: in a
sharp tone   35 **lay eyes on sb.**: see sb.   37 **bewildered**: confused   **crestfallen**:
very disappointed   38 **dodge sth.**: move out of the way of sth.   42 **cave men**:
humans who lived in caves (= Höhlen) a very long time ago   55 **as the saying**
goes: to use a well-known phrase   56 **be meant for one another**: belong together

But before they do it I want you to try and remember what it was like to have been very young.

And particularly the days when you were first in love; when you were like a person sleepwalking, and you didn't quite see the street you were in, and didn't quite hear everything that was said to you. 5

You're just a little bit crazy. Will you remember that, please?

Now they'll be coming out of high school at three o'clock. George has just been elected President of the Junior Class, and as it's June, that means he'll be President of the Senior Class all next year. And Emil's just been elected Secretary and Treasurer. 10

I don't have to tell you how important that is.

He places a board across the backs of two chairs, which he takes from those at the Gibbs family's table. He brings two high stools from the wings and places them behind the board. Persons sitting on the stools will be facing the audience. This is the counter of Mr. Morgan's drugstore. The sounds of young people's 15 voices are heard off left.

Yepp, – there they are coming down Main Street now.

EMILY, *carrying an armful of – imaginary – schoolbooks, comes along Main Street from the left.*

EMILY: I can't, Louise. I've got to go home. Good-by. Oh, Ernestine! 20 Ernestine! Can you come over tonight and do Latin? Isn't that Cicero the worst thing –! Tell your mother you *have* to. G'by. G'by, Helen. G'by Fred.

GEORGE, *also carrying books, catches up with her.*

GEORGE: Can I carry your books home for you, Emily? 25

EMILY: *[Coolly.]* Why … uh … Thank you. It isn't far.

She gives them to him.

GEORGE: Excuse me a minute, Emily. – Say, Bob, if I'm a little late, start practice anyway. And give Herb some long high ones.

EMILY: Good-by Lizzy. 30

GEORGE: Good-By, Lizzy. – I'm awfully glad you were elected, too, Emily.

EMILY: Thank you.

They have been standing on Main Street, almost against the back wall. They
35 *take the first steps toward the audience when* GEORGE *stops and says:*

GEORGE: Emily, why are you mad at me?

EMILY: I'm not mad at you.

GEORGE: You've been treating me so funny lately.

EMILY: Well, since you ask me, I might as well say it right out,
40 George, –

She catches sight of a teacher passing.

Good-by, Miss Corcoran.

GEORGE: Good-by, Miss Corcoran. – Wha – what is it?

EMILY: *[Not scoldingly; finding it difficult to say.]* I don't like the whole
45 change that's come over you in the last year. I'm sorry if that hurts
your feelings, but I've got to – tell the truth and shame the devil.

GEORGE: A change? – Wha – what do you mean?

EMILY: Well, up to a year ago I used to like you a lot. And I used to
watch you as you did everything … because we'd been friends so
50 long … and then you began spending all your time at *baseball* … and
you never stopped to speak to anybody any more. Not even to your
own family you didn't … and, George, it's a fact, you've got awful
conceited and stuck-up, and all the girls say so. They may not say so
to your face, but that's what they say about you behind your back,
55 and it hurts me to hear them say it, but I've got to agree with them a
little. I'm sorry if it hurts your feelings … but I can't be sorry I said
it.

---

4 **sleepwalk**: schlafwandeln   10 **treasurer**: Schatzmeister/in   13 **wings** (pl):
Kulissen   15 **counter**: Tresen   29 **long high one**: (in baseball) hit that sends the
ball long and high   36 **mad at sb.** (AE infml): angry with sb.   44 **scoldingly**:
angrily   46 **shame the devil**: (here) say sth. really bad   53 **conceited** [kən'siːtəd]:
arrogant; having a high opinion of oneself   **stuck-up**: thinking yourself to be better
than others

GEORGE: I ... I'm glad you said it, Emily. I never thought that such a thing was happening to me. I guess it's hard for a fella not to have faults creep into his character.

They take a step or two in silence, then stand still in misery.

EMILY: I always expect a man to be perfect and I think he should be.   5

GEORGE: Oh ... I don't think it's possible to be perfect, Emily.

EMILY: Well, my *father* is, and as far as I can see *your* father is. There's no reason on earth why you shouldn't be, too.

GEORGE: Well, I feel it's the other way round. That men aren't naturally good; but girls are.   10

EMILY: Well, you might as well know right now that I'm not perfect. It's not as easy for a girl to be perfect as a man, because we girls are more – more – nervous. – Now I'm sorry I said all that about you. I don't know what made me say it.

GEORGE: Emily, –   15

EMILY: Now I can see it's not the truth at all. And I suddenly feel that it isn't important, anyway.

GEORGE: Emily ... would you like an ice-cream soda, or something, before you go home?

EMILY: Well, thank you ... I would.   20

They advance toward the audience and make an abrupt right turn, opening the door of Morgan's drugstore. Under strong emotion, EMILY *keeps her face down.* GEORGE *speaks to some passers-by.*

GEORGE: Hello, Stew, – how are you? Good afternoon, Mrs. Slocum.

The STAGE MANAGER, *wearing spectacles and assuming the role of Mr. Morgan,*   25 *enters abruptly from the right and stands between the audience and the counter of his soda fountain.*

STAGE MANAGER: Hello, George. Hello, Emily. – What'll you have? – Why, Emily Webb, – what you been crying about?

GEORGE: *[He gropes for an explanation.]* She ... she just got an awful   30 scare, Mr. Morgan. She almost got run over by that hardware-store wagon. Everybody says that Tom Huckins drives like a crazy man.

STAGE MANAGER: *[Drawing a drink of water.]* Well, now! You take a
    drink of water, Emily. You look all shook up. I tell you, you've got to
35 look both ways before you cross Main Street these days. Gets worse
    every year. – What'll you have?

EMILY: I'll have a strawberry phosphate, thank you, Mr. Morgan.

GEORGE: No, no, Emily. Have an ice-cream soda with me. Two straw-
    berry ice cream sodas, Mr. Morgan.

40 STAGE MANAGER: *[Working the faucets.]* Two strawberry ice-cream
    sodas, yes sir. Yes, sir. There are a hundred and twenty-five horses in
    Grover's Corners this minute I'm talking to you. State Inspector was
    in here yesterday. And now they're bringing in these auto-mo-biles,
    the best thing to do is to just stay home. Why, I can remember when
45 a dog could go to sleep all day in the middle of Main Street and
    nothing come along to disturb him.

He sets the imaginary glasses before them.

    There they are. Enjoy 'em.

He sees a customer, right.

50 Yes, Mrs. Ellis. What can I do for you?

He goes out right.

EMILY: They're so expensive.

GEORGE: No, no, – don't you think of that. We're celebrating our
    election. And then do you know what else I'm celebrating?

55 EMILY: N-no.

GEORGE: I'm celebrating because I've got a friend who tells me all the
    things that ought to be told me.

---

3 **fault**: weakness, bad characteristic   **creep into sth.**: move carefully and quietly
into sth.   4 **misery**: (here) extreme sadness   23 **passer-by**: person passing on
the street   25 **spectacles** (pl; old use): glasses   **assume the role of sb.**: pretend
to be sb.   30 **grope for sth.**: (here) try to think of sth. with difficulty   33 **draw
sth.**: etwas zapfen   34 **all shook up** (AE): very scared or worried   40 **faucet** (AE):
Zapfhahn

EMILY: George, *please* don't think of that. I don' know why I said it. It's
not true. You're –

GEORGE: No, Emily, you stick to it. I'm glad you spoke to me like you
did. But you'll see: I'm going to change so quick – you bet I'm going
to change. And, Emily, I want to ask you a favor.   5

EMILY: What?

GEORGE: Emily, if I go away to State Agriculture College next year, will
you write me a letter once in a while?

EMILY: I certainly will. I certainly will, George …

Pause. They start sipping the sodas through the straws.   10

It certainly seems like being away three years you'd get out of touch
with things. Maybe letters from Grover's Corners wouldn't be so
interesting after a while. Grover's Corners isn't a very important place
when you think of all – New Hampshire; but I think it's a very nice
town.   15

GEORGE: The day wouldn't come when I wouldn't want to know
everything that's happening here. I know *that's* true, Emily.

EMILY: Well, I'll try to make my letters interesting.

Pause.

GEORGE: Y'know. Emily, whenever I meet a farmer I ask him if he thinks   20
it's important to go to Agriculture School to be a good farmer.

EMILY: Why, George –

GEORGE: Yeah, and some of them say that it's even a waste of time. You
can get all those things, anyway, out of the pamphlets the government
sends out. And Uncle Luke's getting old, – he's about ready for me to   25
start in taking over his farm tomorrow, if I could.

EMILY: My!

GEORGE: And, like you say, being gone all that time … in other places
and meeting other people … Gosh, if anything like that can happen
I don't want to go away. I guess new people aren't any better than old   30
ones. I'll bet they almost never are. Emily … I feel that you're as good

a friend as I've got. I don't need to go and meet the people in other towns.

EMILY: But, George, maybe it's very important for you to go and learn all
35   that about – cattle judging and soils and those things. … Of course, I don't know.

GEORGE: *[After a pause, very seriously.]* Emily, I'm going to make up my mind right now. I won't go. I'll tell Pa about it tonight.

EMILY: Why, George, I don't see why you have to decide right now. It's a
40   whole year away.

GEORGE: Emily, I'm glad you spoke to me about that … that fault in my character. What you said was right; but there was *one* thing wrong in it, and that was when you said that for a year I wasn't noticing people, and … you, for instance. Why, you say you were watching me when
45   I did everything … I was doing the same about you all the time. Why, sure, – I always thought about you as one of the chief people I thought about. I always made sure where you were sitting on the bleachers, and who you were with, and for three days now I've been trying to walk home with you; but something's always got in the way.
50   Yesterday I was standing over against the wall waiting for you, and you walked home with *Miss Corcoran*.

EMILY: George! … Life's awful funny! How could I have known that? Why, I thought –

GEORGE: Listen, Emily, I'm going to tell you why I'm not going to
55   Agriculture School. I think that once you've found a person that you're very fond of … I mean a person who's fond of you, too, and likes you enough to be interested in your character … Well, I think that's just as important as college is, and even more so. That's what I think.

---

3 **stick to sth.**: keep doing sth.   24 **pamphlet**: Broschüre   27 **my!**: expression of surprise   35 **cattle judging**: knowing how to check the quality of cows   **soil**: top layer of earth   48 **bleachers** (AE): benches where the spectators can sit during sports events   56 **fond of sb.**: like sb. very much

EMILY: I think it's awfully important, too.

GEORGE: Emily.

EMILY: Y-yes, George.

GEORGE: Emily, if I *do* improve and make a big change … would you be
… I mean: *could* you be …   5

EMILY: I … I am now; I always have been.

GEORGE: *[Pause.]* So I guess this is an important talk we've been
having.

EMILY: Yes … yes.

GEORGE: *[Takes a deep breath and straightens his back.]* Wait just a minute   10
and I'll walk you home.

With mounting alarm he digs into his pockets for the money.

The STAGE MANAGER *enters, right.*

GEORGE, *deeply embarrassed, but direct, says to him:*

Mr. Morgan, I'll have to go home and get the money to pay you for   15
this. It'll only take me a minute.

STAGE MANAGER: *[Pretending to be affronted.]* What's that? George
Gibbs, do you mean to tell me −!

GEORGE: Yes, but I had reasons, Mr. Morgan. − Look, here's my gold
watch to keep until I come back with the money.   20

STAGE MANAGER: That's all right. Keep your watch. I'll trust you.

GEORGE: I'll be back in five minutes.

STAGE MANAGER: I'll trust you ten years, George, − not a day over. −
Got all over your shock, Emily?

EMILY: Yes, thank you, Mr. Morgan. It was nothing.   25

GEORGE: *[Taking up the books from the counter.]* I'm ready.

*They walk in grave silence across the stage and pass through the trellis at the
Webbs' back door and disappear.*

The STAGE MANAGER *watches them go out, then turns to the audience, removing
his spectacles.*   30

STAGE MANAGER: Well, –

He claps his hands as a signal.

Now we're ready to get on with the wedding.

He stands waiting while the set is prepared for the next scene.

35 *Stagehands remove the chairs, tables and trellises from the Gibbs and Webb houses.*

They arrange the pews for the church in the center of the stage. The congregation will sit facing the back wall. The aisle of the church starts at the center of the back wall and comes toward the audience.

40 *A small platform is placed against the back wall on which the Stage Manager will stand later, playing the minister.*

The image of a stained-glass window is cast from a lantern slide upon the back wall.

When all is ready the STAGE MANAGER *strolls to the center of the stage, down* 45 *front, and, musingly, addresses the audience.*

There are a lot of things to be said about a wedding; there are a lot of thoughts that go on during a wedding.

We can't get them all into one wedding, naturally, and especially not into a wedding at Grover's Corners, where they're awfully plain and 50 short.

In this wedding I play the minister. That gives me the right to say a few more things about it.

For a while now, the play gets pretty serious.

---

12 **mounting alarm**: growing anxiety or worry   17 **affronted**: offended, insulted
27 **grave**: serious   37 **pew**: long bench in a church   38 **congregation**: people
gathered in a church   **aisle** [aɪl]: open space down the center of a church
42 **cast an image of sth.**: project a picture   **stained-glass window**: Buntglasfenster
lantern slide: machine for projecting images by shining light on them from behind
45 **musingly**: thoughtfully

Y'see, some churches say that marriage is a sacrament. I don't quite know what that means, but I can guess. Like Mrs. Gibbs said a few minutes ago: People were made to live two-by-two.

This is a good wedding, but people are so put together that even at a good wedding there's a lot of confusion way down deep in people's 5 minds and we thought that that ought to be in our play, too.

The real hero of this scene isn't on the stage at all, and you know who that is. It's like what one of those European fellas said: Every child born into the world is nature's attempt to make a perfect human being. Well, we've seen nature pushing and contriving for some time 10 now. We all know that nature's interested in quantity; but I think she's interested in quality, too, – that's why I'm in the ministry.

And don't forget all the other witnesses at this wedding, – the ancestors. Millions of them. Most of them set out to live two-by-two, also. Millions of them.
15

Well, that's all my sermon. 'Twan't very long, anyway.

The organ starts playing Handel's "Largo."

The congregation streams into the church and sits in silence.

Church bells are heard.

MRS. GIBBS *sits in the front row, the first seat on the aisle, the right section; next* 20 *to her are* REBECCA *and* DR. GIBBS.

Across the aisle MRS. WEBB, WALLY *and* MR. WEBB. *A small choir takes its place, facing the audience under the stained-glass window.*

MRS. WEBB, *on the way to her place, turns back and speaks to the audience.*

MRS. WEBB: I don't know why on earth I should be crying. I suppose 25 there's nothing to cry about. It came over me at breakfast this morning; there was Emily eating her breakfast as she's done for seventeen years and now she's going off to eat it in someone else's house. I suppose that's it.

And Emily! She suddenly said: I can't eat another mouthful, and she 30 put her head down on the table and *she* cried.

She starts toward her seat in the church, but turns back and adds:

Oh, I've got to say it: you know, there's something down-right cruel about sending our girls out into marriage this way.

35 I hope some of her girl friends have told her a thing or two. It's cruel, I know, but I couldn't bring myself to say anything. I went into it blind as a bat myself.

[*In half-amused exasperation.*] The whole world's wrong, that's what's the matter.

40 There they come.

She hurries to her place in the pew.

GEORGE *starts to come down the right aisle of the theatre, through the audience.*

Suddenly three members of his baseball team appear by the right proscenium
45 *pillar and start whistling and catcalling to him. They are dressed for the ball field.*

THE BASEBALL PLAYERS: Eh, George, George! Hast – yaow! Look at him, fellas – he looks scared to death. Yaow! George, don't look so innocent, you old geezer. We know what you're thinking. Don't
50 disgrace the team, big boy. Whoo-oo-oo.

STAGE MANAGER: All right! All right! That'll do. That's enough of that.

Smiling, he pushes them off the stage. They lean back to shout a few more catcalls.

There used to be an awful lot of that kind of thing at weddings in the
55 old days, – Rome, and later. We're more civilized now, – so they say.

---

4 **people are so put together that** …: people are made in such a way that …
12 **ministry**: Priestertum   13 **witness**: Zeuge/in   14 **ancestor**: Vorfahr/in
16 **sermon**: speech by a priest or minister in church   'twan't (non-standard): it was
not   18 **stream**: come or move in quickly   33 **down-right** (AE sl): totally
37 **blind as a bat** (idiom): not seeing or knowing anything about sth.
38 **exasperation**: Verzweiflung   45 **catcall (to) sb.**: call to sb. in a teasing, joking
manner   47 **hast, yaow**: expressions of mockery   49 **geezer**: foolish man
50 **disgrace sb.**: cause sb. to feel shame

The choir starts singing "Love Divine. All Love Excelling –." GEORGE *has reached the stage. He stares at the congregation a moment, then takes a few steps of withdrawal, toward the right proscenium pillar. His mother, from the front row, seems to have felt his confusion. She leaves her seat and comes down the aisle quickly to him.*   5

MRS. GIBBS: George! George! What's the matter?

GEORGE: Ma, I don't want to grow old. Why's everybody pushing me so?

MRS. GIBBS: Why, George ... you wanted it.

GEORGE: No, Ma, listen to me –   10

MRS. GIBBS: No, no, George, – you're a man now.

GEORGE: Listen, Ma, – for the last time I ask you ... All I want to do is to be a fella –

MRS. GIBBS: George! If anyone should hear you! Now stop. Why, I'm ashamed of you!   15

GEORGE: *[He comes to himself and looks over the scene.]* What? Where's Emily?

MRS. GIBBS: *[Relieved.]* George! You gave me such a turn.

GEORGE: Cheer up, Ma. I'm getting married.

MRS. GIBBS: Let me catch my breath a minute.   20

GEORGE: *[Comforting her.]* Now, Ma, you save Thursday nights. Emily and I are coming over to dinner every Thursday night ... you'll see. Ma, what are you crying for? Come on; we've got to get ready for this.

MRS. GIBBS, *mastering her emotion, fixes his tie and whispers to him.*   25

In the meantime, EMILY, *in white and wearing her wedding veil, has come through the audience and mounted onto the stage. She too draws back, frightened, when she sees the congregation in the church. The choir begins: "Blessed Be the Tie That Binds."*

EMILY: I never felt so alone in my whole life. And George over there,   30
looking so ...! I *hate* him. I wish I were dead. Papa! Papa!

MR. WEBB: *[Leaves his seat in the pews and comes toward her anxiously]* Emily! Emily! Now don't get upset. ...

EMILY: But, Papa, – I don't want to get married. ...

35 **MR. WEBB**: Sh-sh-Emily. Everything's all right.

EMILY: Why can' I stay for a while just as I am? Let's go away, –

MR. WEBB: No, no, Emily. Now stop and think a minute.

EMILY: Don't you remember that you used to say, – all the time you used to say – all the time: that I was *your* girl! There must be lots of places
40 we can go to. I'll work for you. I could keep house.

MR. WEBB: Sh ... You mustn't think of such things. You're just nervous, Emily.

He turns and calls:

George! George! Will you come here a minute?

45 *He leads her toward* GEORGE.

Why you're marrying the best young fellow in the world. George is a fine fellow.

EMILY: But Papa, –

MRS. GIBBS *returns unobtrusively to her seat.*

50 MR. WEBB *has one arm around his daughter. He places his hand on* GEORGE'S *shoulder.*

MR. WEBB: I'm giving away my daughter, George. Do you think you can take care of her?

GEORGE: Mr. Webb, I want to ... I want to try. Emily, I'm going to do
55 my best. I love you, Emily. I need you.

EMILY: Well, if you love me, help me. All I want is someone to love me.

GEORGE: I will, Emily, Emily, I'll try.

---

1 **divine**: belonging to or coming from God   **excelling**: going above beyond
everything   16 **come to yourself**: becomes calm   18 **relieved**: no longer feeling
worried   **give sb. a turn**: scare or alarm sb.

EMILY: And I mean for *ever*. Do you hear? For ever and ever.

They fall into each other's arms.

The March from LOHENGRIN *is heard.*

The STAGE MANAGER, *as* CLERGYMAN, *stands on the box, up center.*

MR. WEBB: Come, they're waiting for us. Now you know it'll be all right.   5
Come, quick.

GEORGE *slips away and takes his place beside the* STAGE MANAGER-
CLERGYMAN.

EMILY *proceeds up the aisle on her father's arm.*

STAGE MANAGER: Do you, George, take this woman, Emily, to be your   10
wedded wife, to have …

MRS. SOAMES *has been sitting in the last row of the congregation.*

*She now turns to her neighbors and speaks in a shrill voice. Her chatter
drowns out the rest of the clergyman's words.*

MRS. SOAMES: Perfectly lovely wedding! Loveliest wedding I ever saw.   15
Oh, I do love a good wedding, don't you? Doesn't she make a lovely
bride?

GEORGE: I do.

STAGE MANAGER: Do you, Emily, take this man, George, to be your
wedded husband, –   20

Again his further words are covered by those of MRS. SOAMES.

MRS. SOAMES: Don't know when I've seen such a lovely wedding. But I
always cry. Don't know why it is, but I always cry. I just like to see
young people happy, don't you? Oh, I think it's lovely.

The ring.   25

The kiss.

The stage is suddenly arrested into silent tableau.

The STAGE MANAGER, *his eyes on the distance, as though to himself:*

STAGE MANAGER: I've married over two hundred couples in my day.
Do I believe in it?   30

I don't know.

M. ... marries N. ... millions of them.

The cottage, the go-cart, the Sunday-afternoon drives in the Ford,
the first rheumatism, the grandchildren, the second rheumatism, the
35   deathbed, the reading of the will, –

*He now looks at the audience for the first time, with a warm smile that
removes any sense of cynicism from the next line.*

Once in a thousand times it's interesting.

– Well, let's have Mendelssohn's "Wedding March"!

40   *The organ picks up the March.*

*The bride and groom come down the aisle, radiant, but trying to be very
dignified.*

MRS. SOAMES: Aren't they a lovely couple? Oh, I've never been to such
a nice wedding. I'm sure they'll be happy. I always say: *happiness,*
45   that's the great thing! The important thing is to be happy.

*The bride and groom reach the steps leading into the audience. A bright light
is thrown upon them. They descend into the auditorium and run up the aisle
joyously.*

STAGE MANAGER: That's all the Second Act, folks. Ten minutes'
50   intermission.

Curtain

---

4 **clergyman**: priest, minister   9 **proceed**: move in a particular direction
13 **chatter**: continuous rapid talk about unimportant things   14 **drown sth. out**:
(here) make it impossible to hear sth.   27 **arrested**: stopped   **tableau** ['tæblou]:
(here) unmoving group of people   33 **cottage**: small house   **go-cart**: simple cart
for small children   34 **rheumatism** ['ruːmətɪzm]: Rheuma   35 **will**: Testament
37 **cynicism** ['sɪnɪˌsɪzm]: Zynismus   41 **radiant** ['reɪdiənt]: (here) glowing with
happiness   42 **dignified**: würdevoll

Act III

During the intermission the audience has seen the stagehands arranging the stage. On the right-hand side, a little right of the center, ten or twelve ordinary chairs have been placed in three openly spaced rows facing the audience. These are graves in the cemetery.
Toward the end of the intermission the actors enter and take their places. The 5
front row contains: toward the center of the stage, an empty chair; then MRS. GIBBS; SIMON STIMSON.
The second row contains, among others, MRS. SOAMES.
The third row has WALLY WEBB.
The dead do not turn their heads or their eyes to right or left, but they sit in a 10
quiet without stiffness. When they speak their tone is matter-of-fact, without sentimentality and, above all, without lugubriousness.
The STAGE MANAGER *takes his accustomed place and waits for the house lights to go down.*

STAGE MANAGER: This time nine years have gone by, friends – summer, 15
1913. Gradual changes in Grover's Corners. Horses are getting rarer.

Farmers coming into town in Fords.

Everybody locks their house doors now at night. Ain't been any burglars in town yet, but everybody's heard about 'em.

You'd be surprised, though – on the whole, things don't change 20
much around here.

This is certainly an important part of Grover's Corners. It's on a hilltop – a windy hilltop – lots of sky, lots of clouds, – often lots of sun and moon and stars.

You come up here, on a fine afternoon and you can see range on 25
range of hills – awful blue they are – up there by Lake Sunapee and Lake Winipesaukee ... and way up, if you've got a glass, you can see the White Mountains and Mt. Washington – where North Conway and Conway is. And, of course, our favorite mountain, Mt. Monadnock, 's right here – and all these towns that lie around it: 30
Jaffrey, 'n East Jaffrey, 'n Peterborough, 'n Dublin; and

Then pointing down in the audience.

there, quite a ways down, is Grover's Corners.

Yes, beautiful spot up here. Mountain laurel and li-lacks. I often
35   wonder why people like to be buried in Woodlawn and Brooklyn
when they might pass the same time up here in New Hampshire.

Over there –

Pointing to stage left.

are the old stones, – 1670, 1680. Strong-minded people that come a
40   long way to be independent. Summer people walk around there
laughing at the funny words on the tombstones … it don't do any
harm. And genealogists come up from Boston – get paid by city
people for looking up their ancestors. They want to make sure they're
Daughters of the American Revolution and of the *Mayflower*. … Well,
45   I guess that don't do any harm, either. Wherever you come near the
human race, there's layers and layers of nonsense. …

Over there are some Civil War veterans. Iron flags on their graves …
New Hampshire boys … had a notion that the Union ought to be
kept together, though they'd never seen more than fifty miles of it
50   themselves. All they knew was the name, friends – the United States
of America. The United States of America. And they went and died
about it.

This here is the new part of the cemetery. Here's your friend Mrs.
Gibbs. 'N let me see – Here's Mr. Stimson, organist at the

---

1 **intermission**: pause between the acts of a play   4 **grave**: stone marking where sb.
is buried   **cemetery**: place where the dead are buried   11 **matter-of-fact**: clear and
direct, without expression   12 **lugubriousness** [lə'gu:briəsnəs]: Schwermütigkeit,
Wehmut   27 **glass**: (here) binoculars (= Fernglas)   34 **mountain laurel**: type of
plant   **li-lacks** (non-standard): lilac (= Flieder)   39 **stones**: (here) gravestones
42 **genealogist**: person who researches family histories   44 **Daughters of the
American Revolution**: association of women whose ancestors helped fight for
the independence of the USA   **Mayflower**: boat on which the Pilgrims arrived in
America   47 **Civil War veterans**: soldiers who fought in the American Civil War
(1861–1865)   48 **have a notion that …** (AE): think or believe that sth. …

Congregational Church. And Mrs. Soames who enjoyed the wedding
so – you remember? Oh, and a lot of others. and Editor Webb's boy,
Wallace, whose appendix burst while he was on a Boy Scout trip to
Crawford Notch.

Yes, an awful lot of sorrow has sort of quieted down up here. 5

People just wild with grief have brought their relatives up to this hill.
We all know how it is … and then time … and sunny days … and
rainy days … 'n snow … We're all glad they're in a beautiful place
and we're coming up here ourselves when our fit's over.

Now there are some things we all know, but we don't take'm out and 10
look at'm very often. We all know that *something* is eternal. And it
ain't houses and it ain't names, and it ain't earth, and it ain't even the
stars … everybody knows in their bones that *something* is eternal,
and that something has to do with human beings. All the greatest
people ever lived have been telling us that for five thousand years 15
and yet you'd be surprised how people are always losing hold of it.
There's something way down deep that's eternal about every human
being.

Pause

You know as well as I do that the dead don't stay interested in us 20
living people for very long. Gradually, gradually, they lose hold of the
earth … and the ambition they had … and the pleasures they had …
and the things they suffered … and the people they loved.

They get weaned away from earth – that's the way I put it, – weaned
away. 25

And they stay here while the earth part of 'em burns away, burns out;
and all that time they slowly get indifferent to what's goin' on in
Grover's Corners.

They're waitin'. they're waitin' for something that they feel is comin'.
Something important, and great. Aren't they waitin' for the eternal 30
part in them to come out clear?

Some of the things they're going to say may be'll hurt your feelings –
but that's the way it is: mother 'n daughter … husband 'n wife …
enemy 'n enemy … money 'n miser … all those terribly important

35   things kind of grow pale around here. And what's left when memory's gone, and your identity, Mrs. Smith?

He looks at the audience a minute, then turns to the stage.

Well! There are some *living* people. There's Joe Stoddard, our undertaker, supervising a new-made grave. And here comes a
40   Grover's Corners boy, that left town to go out West.

JOE STODDARD *has hovered about in the background.* SAM CRAIG *enters left, wiping his forehead from the exertion. He carries an umbrella and strolls front.*

SAM CRAIG: Good afternoon, Joe Stoddard.

45   **JOE STODDARD:** Good afternoon, good afternoon. Let me see now: do I know you?

SAM CRAIG: I'm Sam Craig.

JOE STODDARD: Gracious sakes' alive! Of all people! I should'a knowed you'd be back for the funeral. You've been away a long time, Sam.

50   **SAM CRAIG:** Yes, I've been away over twelve years. I'm in business out in Buffalo now, Joe. But I was in the East when I got news of my cousin's death, so I thought I'd combine things a little and come and see the old home. You look well.

JOE STODDARD: Yes, yes, can't complain. very sad, our journey today,
55   Samuel.

SAM CRAIG: Yes.

---

3 **appendix**: Blinddarm   **Boy Scout**: Pfadfinder   5 **sorrow**: extreme unhappiness   6 **grief**: unhappiness felt esp. for sb. who has died   9 **when our fit's over** (non-standard): when we die   11 **eternal**: lasting forever   24 **wean sb. away from sth.**: draw sb. away from sth. (**wean**: abstillen)   34 **miser [pron:]**: sb. who is greedy with money   39 **undertaker**: person responsible for arranging funerals   **supervise sth.**: arrange and direct sth.   41 **hover**: wait in an uncertain manner   42 **exertion**: effort, hard work   48 **Gracious sakes' alive!**: expression of surprise   **I should'a knowed** (non-standard): I should have known   52 **combine sth.**: join or do sth. together

JOE STODDARD: Yes, yes. I always say I hate to supervise when a young person is taken. They'll be here in a few minutes now. I had to come here early today – my son's supervisin' at the home.

SAM CRAIG: [Reading stones.] Old Farmer McCarty, I used to do chores for him – after school. He had the lumbago.   5

JOE STODDARD: Yes, we brought Farmer McCarty here a number of years ago now.

SAM CRAIG: [Staring at Mrs. Gibbs' knees.] Why, this is my Aunt Julia ... I'd forgotten that she'd ... of course, of course.

JOE STODDARD: Yes, Doc Gibbs lost his wife two-three years ago ...   10
about this time. And today's another pretty bad blow for him, too.

MRS. GIBBS: [To Simon Stimson: in an even voice.] That's my sister Carey's boy, Sam ... Sam Craig.

SIMON STIMSON: I'm always uncomfortable when they're around.

MRS. GIBBS: Simon.   15

SAM CRAIG: Do they choose their own verses much, Joe?

JOE STODDARD: No ... not usual. Mostly the bereaved pick a verse.

SAM CRAIG: Doesn't sound like Aunt Julia. There aren't many of those Hersey sisters left now. Let me see: where are ... I wanted to look at my father's and mother's ...   20

JOE STODDARD: Over there with the Craigs ... Avenue F.

SAM CRAIG: [Reading Simon Stimson's epitaph.] He was organist at church, wasn't he? – Hm, drank a lot, we used to say.

JOE STODDARD: Nobody was supposed to know about it. He'd seen a peck of trouble.   25

Behind his hand.

Took his own life, y' know?

SAM CRAIG: Oh, did he?

JOE STODDARD: Hung himself in the attic. They tried to hush it up, but of course it got around. He chose his own epy-taph. You can see it   30
there. It ain't a verse exactly.

SAM CRAIG: Why, it's just some notes of music – what is it?

JOE STODDARD: Oh, I wouldn't know. It was wrote up in the Boston papers at the time.

35 **SAM CRAIG**: Joe, what did she die of?

JOE STODDARD: Who?

SAM CRAIG: My cousin.

JOE STODDARD: Oh, didn't you know? Had some trouble bringing a baby into the world. 'Twas her second, though. There's a little boy
40 'bout four years old.

SAM CRAIG: *[Opening his umbrella.]* The grave's going to be over there?

JOE STODDARD: Yes, there ain't much more room over here among the Gibbses, so they're opening up a whole new Gibbs section over by Avenue B. You'll excuse me now. I see they're comin'.

45 *From left to center, at the back of the stage, comes a procession. Four men carry a casket, invisible to us. All the rest are under umbrellas. One can vaguely see:* DR. GIBBS, GEORGE, *the Webbs, etc. They gather about a grave in the back center of the stage, a little to the left of center.*

MRS. SOAMES: Who is it, Julia?

50 **MRS. GIBBS**: *[Without raising her eyes.]* My daughter-in-law, Emily Webb.

MRS. SOAMES: *[A little surprised, but no emotion.]* Well, I declare! The road up here must have been awful muddy. What did she die of, Julia?

55 **MRS. GIBBS**: In childbirth.

MRS. SOAMES: Childbirth.

---

4 **chore**: small task   5 **lumbago** [lʌmˈbeɪɡoʊ]: Hexenschuss   11 **bad blow for sb.**:
terrible thing to happen to sb.   16 **verses**: short poem on a gravestone
17 **bereaved** [bɪˈriːvd]: relatives and friends of sb. who has died   22 **epitaph**: words
on a gravestone   29 **attic**: Dachboden   **hush sth. up**: keep sth. quiet
30 **epy-taph** (non-standard): epitaph   46 **casket** (AE): coffin   47 **vaguely**: not
clearly   55 **childbirth**: giving birth

Almost with a laugh.

I'd forgotten all about that. My, wasn't life awful –

With a sigh.

and wonderful.

SIMON STIMSON: *[With a sideways glance.]* Wonderful, was it? 5

MRS. GIBBS: Simon! Now, remember!

MRS. SOAMES: I remember Emily's wedding. Wasn't it a lovely wedding! And I remember her reading the class poem at Graduation Exercises. Emily was one of the brightest girls ever graduated from High School. I've heard Principal Wilkins say so time after time. I called on them 10 at their new farm, just before I died. Perfectly beautiful farm.

A WOMAN AMONG THE DEAD: It's on the same road we lived on.

A MAN AMONG THE DEAD: Yepp, right smart farm.

They subside. The group by the grave starts singing "Blessed Be the Tie That Binds." 15

A WOMAN AMONG THE DEAD: I always liked that hymn. I was hopin' they'd sing a hymn.

Pause. Suddenly EMILY *appears from among the umbrellas. She is wearing a white dress. Her hair is down her back and tied by a white ribbon like a little girl. She comes slowly, gazing wonderingly at the dead, a little dazed.* 20

She stops halfway and smiles faintly. After looking at the mourners for a moment, she walks slowly to the vacant chair beside Mrs. Gibbs and sits down.

EMILY: *[To them all, quietly, smiling.]* Hello.

MRS. SOAMES: Hello, Emily. 25

A MAN AMONG THE DEAD: Hello, M's Gibbs.

EMILY: *[Warmly.]* Hello, Mother Gibbs.

MRS. GIBBS: Emily.

EMILY: Hello.

With surprise. 30

It's raining.

Her eyes drift back to the funeral company.

MRS. GIBBS: Yes … They'll be gone soon, dear. Just rest yourself.

35 **EMILY:** It seems thousands and thousands of years since I … Papa remembered that that was my favorite hymn.

Oh, I wish I'd been here a long time. I don' like being new here. – How do you do, Mr. Stimson?

SIMON STIMSON: How do you do, Emily.

40 EMILY *continues to look about her with a wondering smile; as though to shut out from her mind the thought of the funeral company she starts speaking to Mrs. Gibbs with a touch of nervousness.*

EMILY: Mother Gibbs, George and I have made that farm into just the best place you ever saw. We thought of you all the time. We wanted to show you the new barn and a great long ce-ment drinking fountain
45 for the stock. We bought that out of the money you left us.

MRS. GIBBS: I did?

EMILY: Don't you remember, Mother Gibbs – the legacy you left us? Why, it was over three hundred and fifty dollars.

MRS. GIBBS: Yes, yes, Emily.

50 **EMILY:** Well, there's a patent device on the drinking fountain so that it never overflows, Mother Gibbs, and it never sinks below a certain mark they have there, it's fine.

Her voice trails off and her eyes return to the funeral group.

It won't be the same to George without me, but it's a lovely farm.

---

8 **graduation exercises**: ceremony for students who have graduated from high
school   10 **principal** (AE): headmaster   **call on sb.**: visit sb.   13 **right smart
farm** (AE, non-standard): very nice   14 **subside**: (here) become quiet
21 **mourner**: person at a funeral   22 **vacant** ['veɪkənt]: empty   32 **drift**: move
slowly   44 **barn**: Scheune   **ce-ment** (non-standard): cement   50 **patent device**:
patentierte Vorrichtung   51 **overflow**: (of liquid) spill out of its container
53 **trail off**: become quieter

Suddenly she looks directly at Mrs. Gibbs.

Live people don't understand, do they?

MRS. GIBBS: No, dear – not very much.

EMILY: They're sort of shut up in little boxes, aren't they? I feel as though I knew them last a thousand years ago … My boy is spending the day   5
at Mrs. Carter's.

She sees Mr. Carter among the dead.

Oh, Mr. Carter, my little boy is spending the day at your house.

MR. CARTER: Is he?

EMILY: Yes, he loves it there. – Mother Gibbs, we have a Ford, too. Never   10
gives any trouble. I don't drive, though. Mother Gibbs, when does this feeling go away – Of being … one of *them*? How long does it …?

MRS. GIBBS: Sh! dear. Just wait and be patient.

EMILY: *[With a sigh.]* I know. – Look, they're finished. They're going.   15

MRS. GIBBS: Sh–.

The umbrellas leave the stage. DR. GIBBS *has come over to his wife's grave and stands before it a moment.* EMILY *looks up at his face.* MRS. GIBBS *does not raise her eyes.*

EMILY: Look! Father Gibbs is bringing some of my flowers to you. He   20
looks just like George, doesn't he? Oh, Mother Gibbs, I never realized before how troubled and how … how in the dark live persons are. Look at him. I loved him so. From morning till night, that's all they are – troubled.

DR. GIBBS *goes off.*   25

THE DEAD: Little cooler than it was. – Yes, that rain's cooled it off a little. Those northeast winds always do the same thing, don't they? If it isn't a rain, it's a three-day blow. –

A patient calm falls on the stage. The STAGE MANAGER *appears at his proscenium pillar, smoking.* EMILY *sits up abruptly with an idea.*   30

EMILY: But, Mother Gibbs, one can go back; one can go back there again … into living. I feel it. I know it. Why just then for a moment I was thinking about … about the farm … and for a minute I *was* there, and my baby was on my lap as plain as day.

35 MRS. GIBBS: Yes, of course you can.

EMILY: I can go back there and live all those days over again … why not?

MRS. GIBBS: All I can say is, Emily, don't.

EMILY: [*She appeals urgently to the stage manager.*] But it's true, isn't it? I
40 can go and live … back there … again.

STAGE MANAGER: Yes, some have tried – but they soon come back here.

MRS. GIBBS: Don't do it, Emily.

MRS. SOAMES: Emily, don't. It's not what you think it'd be.

45 EMILY: But I won't live over a sad day. I'll choose a happy one – I'll choose the day I first knew that I loved George. Why should that be painful?

They are silent. Her question turns to the stage manager.

STAGE MANAGER: You not only live it; but you watch yourself living it.

50 EMILY: Yes?

STAGE MANAGER: And as you watch it, you see the thing that they – down there – never know. You see the future. You know what's going to happen afterwards.

EMILY: But is that – painful? Why?

55 MRS. GIBBS: That's not the only reason why you shouldn't do it, Emily. When you've been here longer you'll see that our life here is to forget all that, and think only of what's ahead, and be ready for what's ahead. When you've been here longer you'll understand.

---

22 **troubled**: worried, concerned   34 **lap**: Schoß   **as plain as day**: that can be clearly seen   39 **urgent**: eindringlich   45 **live over sth.**: live or experience sth. again   57–58 **what's ahead**: what is to come

EMILY: *[Softly.]* But, Mother Gibbs, how can I *ever* forget that life? It's all I know. It's all I had.

MRS. SOAMES: Oh, Emily. It isn't wise. Really, it isn't.

EMILY: But it's a thing I must know for myself. I'll choose a happy day, anyway.   5

MRS. GIBBS: *No!* – At least, choose an unimportant day. Choose the least important day in your life. It will be important enough.

EMILY: *[To herself.]* Then it can't be since I was married; or since the baby was born.

To the stage manager, eagerly.   10

I can choose a birthday at least, can't I? – I choose my twelfth birthday.

STAGE MANAGER: All right. February 11th, 1899. A Tuesday. – Do you want any special time of day?

EMILY: Oh, I want the whole day.   15

STAGE MANAGER: We'll begin at dawn. You remember it had been snowing for several days; but it had stopped the night before, and they had begun clearing the roads. The sun's coming up.

EMILY: *[With a cry; rising.]* There's Main Street ... why, that's Mr. Morgan's drugstore before he changed it! ... And there's the livery stable.   20

The stage at no time in this act has been very dark; but now the left half of the stage gradually becomes very bright – the brightness of a crisp winter morning. EMILY *walks toward Main Street.*

STAGE MANAGER: Yes, it's 1889. This is fourteen years ago.

EMILY: Oh, that's the town I knew as a little girl. And, *look*, there's the   25 old white fence that used to be around our house. Oh, I'd forgotten that! Oh, I love it so! Are they inside?

STAGE MANAGER: Yes, your mother'll be coming downstairs in a minute to make breakfast.

EMILY: *[Softly.]* Will she?   30

STAGE MANAGER: And you remember: your father had been away for several days; he came back on the early-morning train.

EMILY: No …?

STAGE MANAGER: He'd been back to his college to make a speech – in
35   western New York, at Clinton.

EMILY: Look! There's Howie Newsome. There's our policeman. But he's *dead*; he *died*.

The voices of HOWIE NEWSOME, CONSTABLE WARREN *and* JOE CROWELL, JR. *are heard at the left of the stage.* EMILY *listens in delight.*

40   HOWIE NEWSOME: Whoa, Bessie! – Bessie! 'Morning, Bill.

CONSTABLE WARREN: Morning, Howie.

HOWIE NEWSOME: You're up early.

CONSTABLE WARREN: Been rescuin' a party darn near froze to death, down by Polish Town thar. Got drunk and lay out in the snowdrifts.
45   Thought he was in bed when I shook'm.

EMILY: Why, there's Joe Crowell …

JOE CROWELL: Good morning, Mr. Warren. 'Morning, Howie.

MRS. WEBB *has appeared in her kitchen, but* EMILY *does not see her until she calls.*

50   MRS. WEBB: Chil-*dren*! Wally! Emily! … Time to get up.

EMILY: Mama, I'm here! Oh! how young Mama looks! I didn't know Mama was ever that young.

MRS. WEBB: You can come and dress by the kitchen fire, if you like; but hurry.

55   HOWIE NEWSOME *has entered along Main Street and brings the milk to Mrs. Webb's door.*

Good morning, Mr. Newsome. Whhhh – it's cold.

---

10 **eager**: really wanting sth.   20 **livery stable**: rented stables for horses
22 **crisp**: clear and bright   43 **party** (AE infml): person   **darn near** (AE infml):
very nearly   44 **thar** (AE, non-standard): there   **snowdrift**: pile of snow

HOWIE NEWSOME: Ten below by my barn, Mrs. Webb.

MRS. WEBB: Think of it! Keep yourself wrapped up.

She takes her bottles in, shuddering.

EMILY: *[With an effort.]* Mama, I can't find my blue hair ribbon anywhere. 5

MRS. WEBB: Just open your eyes, dear, that's all. I laid it out for you special – on the dresser, there. If it were a snake it would bite you.

EMILY: Yes, yes …

She puts her hand on her heart. MR. WEBB *comes along Main Street, where he meets* CONSTABLE WARREN. *Their movements and voices are increasingly* 10 *lively in the sharp air.*

MR. WEBB: Good morning, Bill.

CONSTABLE WARREN: Good morning, Mr. Webb. You're up early.

MR. WEBB: Yes, just been back to my old college in New York State. Been any trouble here? 15

CONSTABLE WARREN: Well, I was called up this mornin' to rescue a Polish fella – darn near froze to death he was.

MR. WEBB: We must get it in the paper.

CONSTABLE WARREN: 'Twan't much.

EMILY: *[Whispers.]* Papa. 20

MR. WEBB *shakes the snow off his feet and enters his house.* CONSTABLE WARREN *goes off, right.*

MR. WEBB: Good morning, Mother.

MRS. WEBB: How did it go, Charles?

MR. WEBB: Oh, fine, I guess. I told'm a few things. – Everything all right 25 here?

MRS. WEBB: Yes – can't think of anything that's happened, special. Been right cold. Howie Newsome says it's ten below over to his barn.

MR. WEBB: Yes, well, it's colder than that at Hamilton College. Students'
30 ears are falling off. It ain't Christian. – Paper have any mistakes in
it?

MRS. WEBB: None that I noticed. Coffee's ready when you want it.

He starts upstairs.

Charles! Don't forget, it's Emily's birthday. Did you remember to get
35 her something?

MR. WEBB: *[Patting his pocket.]* Yes, I've got something here.

Calling up the stairs.

Where's my girl? Where's my birthday girl?

He goes off left.

40 **MRS. WEBB:** Don't interrupt her now, Charles. You can see her at break--
fast. She's slow enough as it is. Hurry up, children! It's seven o'clock.
Now, I don't want to call you again.

EMILY: *[Softly, more in wonder than in grief.]* I can't bear it. They're so
young and beautiful. Why did they ever have to get old? Mama, I'm
45 here. I'm grown up. I love you all, everything. – I can't look at
everything hard enough.

*She looks questioningly at the stage manager, saying or suggesting: "Can I go
in?" He nods briefly. She crosses to the inner door to the kitchen, left of her
mother, and as though entering the room, says, suggesting the voice of a girl of
50 twelve:*

Good morning, Mama.

MRS. WEBB: *[Crossing to embrace and kiss her; in her characteristic matter-
of-fact manner.]* Well, now, dear, a very happy birthday to my girl and
many happy returns. There are some surprises waiting for you on the
55 kitchen table .

EMILY: Oh, Mama, you shouldn't have.

---

1 **ten below**: (here) ca. −20 °C   3 **shudder**: shiver due to the cold   54 **many
happy returns**: standard birthday greeting

She throws an anguished glance at the stage manager.

I can't – I can't.

MRS. WEBB: *[Facing the audience, over her stove.]* But birthday or no birthday, I want you to eat your breakfast good and slow. I want you to grow up and be a good strong girl.   5

That in the blue paper is from your Aunt Carrie; and I reckon you can guess who brought the post-card album. I found it on the doorstep when I brought in the milk – George Gibbs ... must have come over in the cold pretty early ... right nice of him.

EMILY: *[To herself.]* Oh, George! I'd forgotten that. ...   10

MRS. WEBB: Chew that bacon good and slow. It'll help keep you warm on a cold day.

EMILY: *[With mounting urgency.]* Oh, Mama, just look at me one minute as though you really saw me. Mama, fourteen years have gone by. I'm dead. You're a grandmother, Mama. I married George Gibbs, Mama.   15
Wally's dead, too. Mama, his appendix burst on a camping trip to North Conway. We felt just terrible about it – don't you remember? But, just for a moment now we're all together Mama, just for a moment we're happy. *Let's look at one another.*

MRS. WEBB: That in the yellow paper is something I found in the attic   20
among your grandmother's things. You're old enough to wear it now, and I thought you'd like it.

EMILY: And this is from you. Why, Mama, it's just lovely and it's just what I wanted. It's beautiful!

She flings her arms around her mother's neck. Her MOTHER *goes on with her*   25
cooking, but is pleased.

MRS. WEBB: Well, I hoped you'd like it. Hunted all over. Your aunt Norah couldn't find one in Concord, so I had to send all the way to Boston.

Laughing.   30

Wally has something for you, too. He made it at manual-training class and he's very proud of it. Be sure you make a big fuss about it.

– Your father has a surprise for you, too; don't know what it is myself. Sh – here he comes.

35 **MR. WEBB:** *[Off stage.]* Where's my girl? Where's my birthday girl?

EMILY: *[In a loud voice to the stage manager.]* I can't. I can't go on. It goes so fast. We don't have time to look at one another.

She breaks down sobbing.

The lights dim on the left half of the stage. Mrs. Webb disappears.

40 I didn't realize. So all that was going on and we never noticed. Take me back – up the hill – to my grave. But first: Wait! One more look.

Good-by, Good-by, world. Good-by, Grover's Corners ... Mama and Papa. Good-by to clocks ticking ... and Mama's sunflowers. And food and coffee. And new-ironed dresses and hot baths ... and
45 sleeping and waking up. Oh, earth, you're too wonderful for anybody to realize you.

She looks toward the stage manager and asks abruptly, through her tears:

Do any human beings ever realize life while they live it? – every, every minute?

50 **STAGE MANAGER:** No.

Pause.

The saints and poets, maybe – they do some.

EMILY: I'm ready to go back.

She returns to her chair beside Mrs. Gibbs.

55 *Pause.*

MRS. GIBBS: Were you happy?

EMILY: No ... I should have listened to you. That's all human beings are! Just blind people.

---

1 **anguished**: painful and unhappy   11 **chew sth.**: etwas kauen   25 **fling sth.**: throw sth.   27 **hunt all over (for sth.)**: look everywhere for sth.   31 **manual-training class**: (here) woodwork or metalwork class   32 **make a big fuss about sth.**: be very excited about sth.   38 **sob**: cry

MRS. GIBBS: Look, it's clearing up. The stars are coming out.

EMILY: Oh, Mr. Stimson, I should have listened to them.

SIMON STIMSON: *[With mounting violence; bitingly.]* Yes, now you know.
Now you know! That's what it was to be alive. To move about in a
cloud of ignorance; to go up and down trampling on the feelings of   5
those ... of those about you. To spend and waste time as though you
had a million years. To be always at the mercy of one self-centered
passion, or another. Now you know – that's the happy existence you
wanted to go back to. Ignorance and blindness.

MRS. GIBBS: *[Spiritedly.]* Simon Stimson, that ain't the whole truth and   10
you know it. Emily, look at that star, I forget its name.

A MAN AMONG THE DEAD: My boy Joel was a sailor, – knew 'em all.
He'd set on the porch evenings and tell 'em all by name. Yes, sir,
wonderful!

ANOTHER MAN AMONG THE DEAD: A star's mighty good company.   15

A WOMAN AMONG THE DEAD: Yes. Yes, 'tis.

SIMON STIMSON: Here's one of *them* coming.

THE DEAD: That's funny. 'Tain't no time for one of them to be here. –
Goodness sakes.

EMILY: Mother Gibbs, it's George.   20

MRS. GIBBS: Sh, dear. Just rest yourself.

EMILY: It's George.

GEORGE *enters from the left, and slowly comes toward them.*

A MAN FROM AMONG THE DEAD: And my boy, Joel, who knew the
stars – he used to say it took millions of years for that speck o' light   25
to git to the earth. Don't seem like a body could believe it, but that's
what he used to say – millions of years.

GEORGE *sinks to his knees then falls full length at Emily's feet.*

A WOMAN AMONG THE DEAD: Goodness! That ain't no way to behave!

MRS. SOAMES: He ought to be home.   30

EMILY: Mother Gibbs?

MRS. GIBBS: Yes, Emily?

EMILY: They don't understand, do they?

MRS. GIBBS: No, dear. They don't understand.

35 *The* STAGE MANAGER *appears at the right, one hand on a dark curtain which he slowly draws across the scene.*

In the distance a clock is heard striking the hour very faintly.

STAGE MANAGER: Most everybody's asleep in Grover's Corners. There are a few lights on: Shorty Hawkins, down at the depot, has just
40 watched the Albany train go by. And at the livery stable somebody's setting up late and talking. – Yes, it's clearing up. There are the stars – doing their old, old crisscross journeys in the sky. Scholars haven't settled the matter yet, but they seem to think there are no living beings up there. Just chalk … or fire. Only this one is straining away,
45 straining away all the time to make something of itself. The strain's so bad that every sixteen hours everybody lies down and gets a rest.

He winds his watch.

Hm. … eleven o'clock in Grover's Corners. – You get a good rest, too. Good night.

THE END

---

5 **trample on sth.**: damage sth. by walking on it   7 **be at the mercy of sth.**: be controlled by sth.   **self-centered**: selfish   8 **passion**: Leidenschaft   10 **spirited**: excited   13 **set** (non-standard pron): sit   **porch**: veranda   25 **speck o' light** (AE): small light   26 **a body** (AE): a person, someone

Information about the Play

Overview

Thornton Wilder, Pulitzer Prize-winning, internationally acclaimed novelist, entered the decade of the 1930s determined to achieve still another great distinction: playwright in full Broadway standing. He appeared to have achieved this dream on Friday evening, February 4, 1938, at Henry Miller's Theatre on Forty-third Street, when Frank Craven, the admired character actor, played the part of the Stage Manager in the premiere of *Our Town*, directed and produced by the legendary Jed Harris. The play concluded with the language used in this production: "They're resting in Grover's Corners. Tomorrow's going to be another day. Good night to you, too. Good night. Get a good rest." After a short, stunned silence, broken by audible sniffles in the house, the audience offered an ovation.

The next day, the phone rang off the hook with good news at the author's home ninety miles away in Hamden, Connecticut. A particularly informative call came from Wilder's greatest actor friend, Ruth Gordon, then starring as Nora in Wilder's translation of Ibsen's *Doll's House*, also playing on Broadway and also directed by Harris. (It is forgotten that Wilder had two shows running in New York City at the same time in 1938.) Wilder reported the highlights of Gordon's call (especially the detail about tears in the eyes of a Hollywood mogul) to Dwight Dana, his attorney, confidant, and keeper of Wilder's exchequer during the Great Depression. This letter is the earliest written record of the playwright's reaction to a theatrical opening that would have a defining influence on his reputation ever after. "Dear Dwight," he began:

Funny thing's happened.
Ruth phoned down. It's already broken a house record.
In spite of the mixed reviews when the box-office opened Saturday morning there were 26 people in line; the line continued all day, and the police had to close it for ten minutes so that the audience

30   could get into the matinee; and that $6,500 was taken in on that
      day – the two performances and the advanced sale.
      Imagine that!
      Friday night both Sam Goldwyn and Bea Lillie were seen to be
      weeping. Honest! …
35   Isn't it astonishing, and fun and exhausting?

Our Town did indeed receive mixed reviews. Negative comments focused
on whether it was "dramatic" enough to be called a play or merely what
Robert Benchley in *The New Yorker* saw as "so much ersatz." John
Gassner in *One Act Play Magazine* dismissed the play as "devoid of
40   developed situations" and thus much less than "a major dramatic
experience," and George Jean Nathan later called it "a stunt." *Time*
thought that Wilder's effective use of "Chinese methods gives ten times
as much 'theatre' as conventional scenery could give," but nevertheless
found the third act full of disappointing "mysticism and high-flown
45   speculation." The *New Masses*, the left-wing journal, whose editor,
Michael Gold, had famously trashed Wilder's fiction earlier in the
decade, tipped its hat slightly to the work while delivering a salvo: "It is
an exasperating play, hideous in its basic idea and beautiful in its writing,
acting and staging." ("Hideous" was the playwright's favorable treatment
50   of middle-class, bourgeois values and lives.)
      But where it really mattered, in such papers as the *Herald-Tribune*,
the *World-Telegram*, the *Brooklyn Daily Eagle*, and even in the tabloid
Sunday Mirror, the play's staging, acting, directing, and themes evoked
powerful adjectives and praise. It was "beautiful," "touching," "one of
55   the great plays of our day," "magnificent." Robert Colman in the *Mirror*
pulled out all stops, proclaiming it "worthy of an honored place in any
anthology of the American drama," as soon it would be, starting in 1940.
Brooks Atkinson in the *New York Times*, the first among equals in
influence, wrote a review of poetic intensity, hailing Wilder and Harris

---

13 **ring off the hook**: (of a telephone) ring constantly   16 **Henrik Ibsen**
(1826–1906): Norwegian playwright   20 **Hollywood mogul**: important and
powerful movie producer   33 **Sam Goldwyn**: famous Hollywood studio boss in
the 1930s   47 **salvo**: attack

for a play that "transmuted the simple events of human life into universal reverie," and that contained nothing less than "a fragment of the immortal truth."

By February 14, box-office sales having held up well enough to justify moving the play to its permanent home, the Morosco Theater, Wilder felt comfortable enough to write to his friend Lady Sibyl Colfax in London: "Lord! I can't believe it myself. It's the hit of the town. Almost everybody's got some reservations against it (including myself) but everybody's discussing it and going to see it."

The drama that made even Sam Goldwyn cry appears as "M Marries N" in a list of ideas for plays penned July 2, 1935. This precise language – is it possibly the *oldest* in the play? – survives in the final version, at the the end of Act II, when the Stage Manager, as minister, says: "M. ... marries N. ... millions of them." This "alphabet" marriage appears less than two weeks after Wilder encountered, at his brother's wedding in New Jersey, the custom of the groom not seeing his bride on the wedding day until they meet at the church. This fact has always made *Our Town* an unusually personal (and tearful) experience for his family.

Thanks to records, we know that "M Marries N" evolved into "Our Village" in 1936, and into "Our Town" by 1937. Wilder was a writer who could not do serious writing in familiar settings. It is no surprise, therefore, that *Our Town*'s creative journey encompassed transatlantic streamers; writing tables in hotels and hideaways in such varied places as the Caribbean island of St. Lucia (October 1936) and the MacDowell Colony in Peterborough, New Hampshire (June 1937); and such addresses in Switzerland in the fall of 1937 as Zurich, St. Moritz, Sils-Maria, Sils-Baselgia, Ascona, and Ruschlikon. Of these, the Veltin Studio at the MacDowell Colony and especially a room in the Hotel Belvoir in Ruschlikon (a small village outside Zurich – eight francs a day, including breakfast and lunch) were key locations where scenes and acts were written, discarded, and revised. And rain or shine, there was one other central ingredient in a Wilder writing day – a long walk. Those taken in the Peterborough and Lake Sunapee areas of New Hampshire, starting in 1923, set the stage in his mind for *Our Town*. Shortly after the play opened, Wilder quantified his walks in an interview: "At a rough guess, one day's walk is productive of one fifteen-minute scene. Everything I've

ever done has come into being that way and I don't think I could work
out an entire play or novel at a desk now if I tried."

40 The following excerpts from Wilder's letters open helpful windows
on the author's progress during the key summer months of 1937. As
they indicate, he was, in this period, working on several plays at once.
(A reading below touches on the importance of Wilder's one-act plays of
1931 as the tool chest he used to construct *Our Town*, among them *The
Happy Journey to Trenton and Camden* and *Pullman Car Hiawatha*.)

45 *June 24 from the MacDowell Colony to Alexander Woollcott.*
My darts thrown at perfection are being feathered and pointed in
many tranquil hours in these woods. Three of them are being
assembled at once. None are ready to leave behind me when I
sail. I always think of Our Village as yours. It is intended to give
50 you pleasure. The Happy Journey [*to Trenton and Camden*] is no
longer part of it. The last act in the cemetery will be prodigious.
[*Our Town* is dedicated to Woollcott, the critic and broadcaster.
He included *The Happy Journey* in the 1935 edition of his
influential *Woollcott Reader.*]

55 *September 4 from Zurich to his family.*
I've begun the Second Act of "Our Town." It'll be awful hard to
combine all the things, general and particular, that one would
wish to say about love and marriage, – combine them in one long
flowing musical curve. ... And back into the First Act go some
60 preparatory speeches: Amy "Mama, am I ... am I nice lookin'?"
Mother "Oh, go-on-with-you. All my children got good features.
I'd be ashamed if they hadn't." [Amy was an earlier name for
Emily.]

September 6 to Sibyl Colfax from Zurich.
65 A scene that must not be morbid though it plunges deep in the
unconfessed structure of the mind. The bride seems never to have
seen the groom before, is terrified, fears him, appeals to the

---

46 **throw darts at perfection**: attempt to produce sth. perfect

audience for help, draws her father over to the proscenium pillar, and asks him to run away with her to the South Sea, to anywhere. He too is haunted; over her head tells the audience that no girl should be married, that there is no anxious state in the world crueler than that of a young wife … then passes his hand over his forehead and trembling, reassures his daughter and leads her back to the clergyman.

September 22 to family from Sils-Baselgia.
Wonderful place.
The great ghost of Nietzsche. … Last night my play got such an influx of new ideas that now it's the most beautiful play you can imagine.

September 25 to Sibyl Colfax from Zurich.
It's raining and the pantomime of the funeral goes on over in a far corner of the stage and there are ten umbrellas up.
Every act has hymn-singing in it – the choir practice, the wedding, the funeral. And when the city-dwelling Americans get those homely ur-American hymns going through them, – Just as the negro spirituals bathed and supported "Green pastures."
Yes, the last act has lots of cold iron and grasping-the-nettle in it, but Sils-Maria gave it an ultimate Affirming Ring.

October 1 to Sibyl Colfax from Ruschlikon.
I'm behind schedule. I had hoped on October first to be able to jump to Play No #2.
But it doesn't matter: "Our Town's" First and Second Acts are all fair-copied and I think "set." And that difficult cactus-spined third is moving into place every day.
Lord! What I got myself in for. A theologico-metaphysico-transcription from the Purgatorio with panels of American rural genre-stuff.
Isn't it awful?
While they are waiting there to have the Earth slip from them, does Dante's vesperal angel make its appearance?

Can we see by the turning of their heads, by a *recuillement* that
35   Something has come?
First of all: do I believe it?

October 28 to family from Ruschlikon.
Jed [Harris] telephoned from London for 20 minutes the other
night. He wants to know if "Our Town" would be a good play for
40   the Xmas season in New York. Would it?!! And guess who might
act the lanky tooth-picking stage-manager? Sinclair Lewis! He's
been plaguing Jed to let him act for a long time; and there's a part
for his famous New England parlor-trick monologues. Don't tell
anybody anything about it. [Lewis played the Stage Manager later
45   in summer stock.]

November 24 to Amy Wertheimer from Paris.
I was summoned by Jed Harris to Paris and read him "Our Town"
– a New Hampshire village explored by the techniques of Chinese
Drama and of <u>Pullman Car Hiawatha</u>. He was very enthusiastic
50   and hurried home to America to put it on for the Xmas season. ...
I follow soon for rehearsals.

Wilder did not, in fact, finish *Our Town* in Europe, and no walks are
recorded in the last two places associated with the completion of the
acting script. To assure that end *and* get publicity for it, Harris snatched
55   Wilder off the dock when he arrived home on the *Queen Mary* and
imprisoned him on Long Island. (To quote one headline: WILDER LOCKED
UP TILL HE FINISHES THAT PLAY OF HIS.) The prison, a cottage on Long
Island in the swanky Cold Spring Harbor area, came with amenities,
including cook and butler and much chintz.

---

10 **Friedrich Nietzsche**: German philosopher   19 **spiritual**: type of religious
song sung by blacks   29 **Purgatorio**: part of the Divine Comedy by the Italian
poet Dante (1265–1321) which depicts purgatory (= Fegefeuer)   33 **vesperal**:
evening   34 **recuillement** (French): awareness, realization   41 **Sinclair Lewis**
(1884–1951): American novelist who satirized small-town American life
58 **swanky**: chic, fashionable   59 **chintz**: (here) expensive furnishing

More spartan was the spot where Wilder finally completed the acting
script on November 19, only a few days before rehearsals began: the
Columbia University Club on Forty-third Street, three blocks from
Broadway. Writing to Dwight Dana, he coupled this good news with a
distressing report that he had not yet signed a play contract with Jed   5
Harris, with whom he was "in such a mess of friendship-collaboration
sentiment … and with a sense of sense of guilt about the unfinished
condition of the play that I can't pull myself together to insist." But what
of Our Town's prospects? Wilder reported that Frank Craven (who had a
contract) thought it "a possibility that the play will be a smashing   10
success." This feeling built among the cast and the few people admitted
to observe rehearsals (they predicted "big things"), although Wilder was
almost immediately discouraged by some of Harris's stage directions,
and worst of all, his "tasteless additions" to Wilder's script. These
irritations soon grew into a violent quarrel that poisoned their   15
relationship.

Our Town's route to Broadway wound through Princeton and Boston.
The premiere was a single performance at the McCarter Theatre in
Princeton, New Jersey, on January 22, 1938. The play drew a ferociously
negative review in Variety ("it will probably go down as the season's most   20
extravagant waste of fine talent"), but others saw it the way Wilder did
when he wrote to Dana:

> The performance at Princeton was an undoubted success. The
> large theatre was sold out with standees. Take was 1900 dollars;
> Audience swept by laughter often; astonishment; and lots of tears;   25
> long applause at the end by an audience that did not move from
> its seats.

Boston was in some ways a very different story. Our Town arrived there
for a scheduled two-week run at the Wilbur Theater starting Tuesday,
January 25. It is popularly believed that the Boston critics panned the   30
play. In Fanfare (1957), the legendary stage publicist Richard Maney
paints this standard story as only a New Yorker can: "[The play's]
reception was so chilly and attendance so wretched that the two-week
engagement was pared to one. The American Athens wanted no truck

35 with a play without scenery. To Beacon Hill Brahmins, such an omission
was as confusing as tackling a grapefruit without a spoon."

Business was terrible at the Wilbur in Boston in 1938, as it was in
other theaters in that especially difficult Great Depression year. But the
reviews were not all pans. Wilder described them as "cautious but not
40 unfavorable." Critics saw much to like in the play, but they were
perplexed and mystified by its avant-garde features, as this lead from an
Associated Press story suggests: SPEECH-MAKING BY 'CORPSES' UNUSUAL
FEATURE. Mordaunt Hall of the *Boston Evening Transcript*, a prominent
voice, found the play "curious," but noted that it was "roundly applauded
45 by last night's gathering." A *New York Times* piece painted a similar
picture – a "puzzled" audience but one that nevertheless at the end
"applauded unashamedly a touching, delicately written, warmly acted
play that bears a distant resemblance in its technique to Chinese or
Greek methods translated into New England terms."

50 In Boston, *Our Town* drew perhaps the most extraordinary headline
in its history. In what Wilder described as a "bomb dropped on the cast,"
the day before the Boston opening Harris's companion, the actress
Rosamond Pinchot, committed suicide at her home outside New York.
The tragedy was reported on page 1 in the *Boston Post* January 25:

55

LINK SUICIDE TO NEW SHOW HERE

Rosamond Pinchot Said to Have Been Brooding

Over Failure to Win Part in "Our Town"

Whatever the differences between the sizes of the houses, the Princeton
and Boston productions shared one similarity – tears. Now disturbed
60 about the audience's reaction to the play, Wilder wrote to Sibyl Colfax:

Audiences heavily papered. Laughed and cried. The wife of the
Governor of Mass took it on her self to telephone the box-office

---

20 **Variety**: influential show business newspaper   30 **pan sth.**: give sth. a very
bad review   35 **Beacon Hill Brahmins**: (here) the rich and educated people of
Boston   61 **papered**: (here) given free tickets to fill a performance   62 **Mass**:
Massachusetts

that the last act was too sad. She was right. Such sobbing and
nose-blowing you never heard. Matinee audience, mostly women,
emerged red-eyed, swollen faced, and mascara-stained. I never
meant that; and direction is responsible for much of it; Jed is now
wildly trying to sweeten and water-down the text.   5

Shaken by Pinchot's death, the poor attendance, and critics who refused
to leap with excitement, and losing significant money, Harris faced three
options for a drama in which he had complete faith: close it (which he
prepared to do); withdraw it for further work and try it out in another
city (an idea apparently entertained, however briefly, with New Haven   10
in mind); or arrange an earlier-than-planned New York opening. Harris
chose the last, threw the cast into four days of rehearsals, and opened
the play temporarily at Henry Miller's Theatre on Friday, February 4.
Said to have tipped the balance toward that option were the opinions of
several influential figures who came from New York to see the play,   15
among them the playwright Marc Connelly. He declared *Our Town*
"magnificent," and ready for Broadway. Wilder, now suffering physical
symptoms of distress from the tension of it all, wrote Sibyl Colfax as
rehearsals began in New York: "Marc [Connelly] and other have sent the
rumors around N.Y. that Friday night will be one exciting occasion. Jed 20
is charging $ 5.50 top, which is insane."

As noted, the *Our Town* opening was an exciting occasion. The original
Broadway production did not, however, break records. Brooks Atkinson
would recall in 1973 that had it not received the Pulitzer Prize in May
1938, four months into the run, "it might have relapsed into the yawning 25
obscurity of those innumerable Broadway plays that never really
succeeded." To keep the production going during the difficult hot
summer months, Wilder accepted royalty cuts that reached 50 percent.
Business improved somewhat when he played the part of the Stage
Manager for two weeks in September. The job earned him respectable   30
kudos in the press. He also enjoyed himself, although the experience
left him "alternately exhausted and dizzy."

On November 19, slightly more than ten months into the run, Harris
closed *Our Town* in New York after 336 performances and took it out on
what was projected to be a lengthy national tour. Three months and   35

twelve cities later, on February 11, 1939, the tour ended abruptly in Chicago. Thomas Coley, an original cast member, recalled the reason in a memoir: "Jed noticed that Frank Craven was earning more each week than he, the producer-director. He came out to persuade Mr. Craven to
40 reduce his percentage of the gross. They argued. Jed lost. In a rage, he closed the play, thus cutting off the nose to spite his face, and, incidentally, the noses of forty-seven actors plus the crew."

Although *Our Town* had a less than record-breaking launch, its subsequent hostory, measured in amateur and stock productions, earned
45 it the "smashing success" that Craven had predicted on the eve of rehearsals. And it all happened quite quickly.

The play's amateur and stock rights, for example, became available for the first time on April 19, 1939. By December 31, 1940, the play (handled by Samuel French) had been performed on amateur stages in
50 no fewer than 795 communities. The figure represented every state of the Union save one (Rhode Island), as well as the District of Columbia, Hawaii, and four Canadian provinces. This laid the foundation for the *Our Town* rule of thumb ever since: It is performed at least once each night somewhere in this country. Behind these figures lies a play that has
55 marvelous parts for young people, is not expensive to mount, is glorious to teach, and treats life, death, and love in such an immediate fashion as to leave indelible and typically nostalgic impressions on generations of students.

Our Town was also a hit from the beginning with stock companies.
60 Through May 1944 it had already been performed forty-three times, principally in the era's summer theaters in New England and the mid-Atlantic states. Five of these productions featured Wilder as the Stage Manager. Since World War II, the pattern has continued, now tied to the growth of American regional theaters in the postwar period. Between
65 1970 and 1999, for example, the play was performed ninety-one times in professional stock and regional theaters across the country, and it has already been performed another sixteen times so far in the new century. The Long Wharf Theatre in New Haven, Connecticut, Wilder's home

---

25–26 **yawning obscurity**: totale Vergessenheit   31 **kudos** (Greek): praise
44 **stock production**: Repertoire einer Theatergruppe

city, mounted the play's fiftieth-anniversary production, starring Hal Holbrook. Another landmark production occurred in 1976, at the Williamstown Summer Festival, when Geraldine Fitzgerald bowed as the first woman to play the Stage Manager.

Marc Connelly, one of the saviors of the play when it stumbled in 5 Boston, played the Stage Manager when *Our Town* had its first major New York revival in 1944, a production Jed Harris directed. There have been four revivals since, the last two being Lincoln Center's Tony Award-winning production starring Spalding Gray in 1988 and the Westport Country Playhouse's successful production starring Paul Newman in 10 2002. These first-class and/or stock productions routinely provide the opportunity for audiences, critics, and artists to explore the play and its artistry in a fresh way. The findings can be revelatory – witness playwright Lanford Wilson writing about the fiftieth-anniversary production in 1987 in the *New York Times*; "And where the hell did [Wilder] get the 15 reputation for being soft? Let's agree never to say that again. Let's not be blinded by the homey cute surface from the fact that 'Our Town' is a deadly cynical and acidly accurate play." After September 11, theaters saw in it what Richard Hamburger at the Dallas Theater center spoke of as a reassuring "sense of continuity and community." 20

Our Town has also been an international success story, beginning with the first productions in 1938 in the Scandinavian countries. Isabel Wilder's letter to her brother Amos in the Readings that follow opens a small window onto a large story, itself a reminder that the play's themes, seemingly so American, have universal appeal. For example, since 1960, 25 *Unsere kleine Stadt* has been produced in at least twenty-two languages in twenty-seven countries, outside of Germany, and translated and almost certainly performed in more. (Precise figures can be hard to come by in this chapter of *Our Town's* history.) Germany has always been a special case for this play as well as Wilder's other works. Between 1950 30 and 1970, *Our Town* was produced professionally eighty times in Germany; although it is done less often now, it continues to be performed and widely read in schools. It says much about the drama's planetary appeal and vision that the cover of the new German paperback edition depicts a major metropolis. 35

Despite many requests, Wilder did not permit *Our Town* to be fashioned into a live musical. But he was open to other options.

Forgotten is the play's extensive radio history, launched in March 1938
with a segment of *The Kate Smith Hour* (then the nation's most popular
40 radio show) and including a six-month Camel Caravan series during
World War II, and Wilder's own appearance in a *Theatre Guild on the Air*
broadcast in September 1946. With one notable exception the play's
early record in television is also forgotten. The exception is the ninety-
minute musical version in 1955 starring Frank Sinatra, remembered
45 because of the continuing popularity of the award-winning Sammy
Cahn–James Van Heusen song "Love and Marriage." In 1977, Hal
Holbrook played the lead role in an admired two-hour NBC broadcast,
a tradition of televising the "straight play" that the productions with
Spalding Gray and Paul Newman have built upon since.
50   Thanks to cable televison, movie cassettes, and DVD, the *Our Town*
movie released by Sol Lesser at a huge celebration in Boston in May
1940 continues to have a public presence. (This time, *Our Town* was a
success in that city.) Wilder, who had credentials as a screenwriter, was
not initially interested in any participation in the script. But to protect
55 his increasingly valuable property, he became deeply involved in it,
including the famous decision to let Emily live (she dies only in a
dream). He expressed his view on the matter this way in a letter to Lesser
(thereby providing countless students with a term-paper subject):

I've always thought [Emily should live]. In a movie you see the
60   people so close to that a different relation is established. In the
theatre they are halfway abstractions in an allegory; in the movie
they are very concrete. So in so far as the play is a Generalized
Allegory she dies – we die – they die; in so far as it's a Concrete
Happening it's not important that she die. Let her live – the idea
65   will have been imparted anyway.

A month after the Broadway opening Wilder had fled to Arizona to
complete *The Merchant of Yonkers*, a second play that had made the
earlier trip to Switzerland. It is clear from letters that he was thinking

---

13 **witness sth.**: (here) see as an example   33 **planetary**: universal   65 **impart
sth.**: pass on sth. (e.g. information)

hard about what he had learned about playwriting from his *Our Town* experience. He credited Jed Harris for much of its success, and would approach him two more times to direct new plays. (Harris passed.) But it is also clear that he never believed Harris fully grasped the deeper meaning of his play. In March 1938, from Arizona, he wrote his sister an   5 opinion he appears never to have changed. The immediate context was that Eleanor Roosevelt had written a day earlier in her column "My Day" that the play had "depressed her beyond words."

> I've now decided that on one plane Our Town is a very pessimistic
> piece. But on a higher plane it isn't. That's where Jed fell down. If   10
> you hang the planets and the years high up above the play, you
> can get the Reconciliation but if you don't it's crushing. Jed
> gypped me on "the cosmic overtones" just where [Max] Reinhardt
> would be best.

Less than a year later, Reinhardt, the great German director whom   15 Wilder had idealized since boyhood, took *Merchant* to Broadway – and failed dismally. After the war, the play was reborn as *The Matchmaker* and set a Wilder Broadway record of 486 performances, 110 more than *Our Town*. To quote Wilder (and many others): "Theater is a funny business."   20

In the end, the "funny business" that Wilder sought to conquer after 1930 blessed him with great artistic and monetary success. Where *Our Town* is concerned, one can go further. Thornton Wilder had two sensational moments in his lifetime – one in fiction, *The Bridge of San Luis Rey*, and one in drama, *Our Town*. Had he been a baseball player,   25 they could be compared to hitting grand slams in the bottom of the ninth with his team three runs down.

Sensations cast long shadows. *Our Town*'s shadow is especially long and deep. It is the grand slam at the last out of the last game of the World Series. It says much about the author's drive and his sense of   30 himself that the play's success did not cripple his art; Wilder was incapable of resting on laurels. He went on to write more plays and novels, including another Pulitzer Prize-winning drama and a novel that received the National Book Award, and busied himself to the day of his death with such a host of other literary deeds that he earned among the   35 cognoscenti the reputation as a man of letters rather than only a novelist or a playwright.

But the *Our Town* shadow was long and deep – and remains so. When Wilder's turn came in 1997 to end up on a stamp, the artist did not hesitate to depict him against the backdrop of a New England landscape. The sun is setting and soon the village will be set against "the life of the stars." That is where Thornton Wilder rests.

Wilder Interviewed

Six weeks before the Princeton opening, Harris let Wilder out of "prison" on Long Island to be interviewed for an article published on December 7, 1937, in the *New York World-Telegram*, from which this excerpt is taken. Wilder characteristically ranges over his calling, the nature and appeal of drama as an art form for the times, and the nature of his own play. *A Doll's House* opened in New York on January 27 and set a Broadway record for the work (144 performances). To write drama full-time, Wilder had given up his teaching post at the University of Chicago in 1936.

Jed Harris (Yale '21) has Thornton Wilder (Yale '21) under lock and key out Port Washington way. This is because Professor Wilder has to finish an original play called *Our Town* which Mr. Harris is waiting to put into rehearsal.

Every other day or so, however, Mr. Harris lets Mr. Wilder come to town (under surveillance); and in town he was today, pacing about Mr. Harris' office in the Empire Theater Building.

You may know Mr. Wilder as "the professor," or as "the man who wrote *The Bridge of San Luis Rey*," but Mr. Wilder, from now on, wants to be known as Mr. Wilder, the dramatist.

---

13 **gyp sb.**: fail or cheat sb.   32 **rest on (your) laurels**: live on the praise of past achievements   36 **cognoscenti** (Italian): people who know (i.e. who are well-educated)   46 **range over sth.**: (here) talk about sth.

Gene Tunney's former walking companion is a short, pleasant man, shyly articulate, a trifle pedagogic. His brown hair has deserted the regions above his capacious forehead and gone gray at the temples; his blue eyes look out earnestly from behind horn-rimmed spectacles; his fingers, thin and tapered, enlace themselves   5
on the desk before him as he talks.

The author of – in addition to *The Bridge* – *The Woman of Andros* and *Heaven's My Destination* is not exactly making his theatrical debut. Some years ago the town saw his translation of M. André Obey's *Le Viol de Lucrèce*; he has written a quartet of one-acters   10
and an adaptation of Ibsen's *A Doll's House*, abetted by the incomparable Ruth Gordon as Nora, is even now hovering in Chicago preparatory to a descent upon Manhattan. Nevertheless: "I feel," says Mr. Wilder, "that my whole life has been an apprenticeship to writing for the theater.   15

"You see (eagerly) imaginative story telling consists of telling a number of lies in order to convey a truth; it is a rearrangement of falsehoods which, if it is done honestly, results in verity.

"Now, the thing which most appeals to me about the theater is the absence of editorial comment. There is arrangement, of   20
course, but at least you do not have in the theater, as in the novel, a single fallible human being claiming Godlike omniscience.

"To be sure, it is something of an illusion, but I regard it as a great good."

Mr. Wilder leaned back in his chair, lit another cigarette and went   25
on. One felt as though one were in an especially pleasant classroom.

"Another thing. It is always now on the stage. The stage lives in the pure present, it offers always the pure action and not someone's digestion of that action. ...   30

"The play – well, you might say that it is kind of an attempt at complete immersion into everything about a New Hampshire village which, I hope, is gradually felt by the audience to be an allegorical representation of all life.

"It is an idea which has teased me for a long while, but you could   35
say that it was really done – most of it – last summer in a little hotel near Zurich.

"You know, I'm a Wisconsin boy from State of Maine stock, but I
spent six summers tutoring in a New Hampshire camp and six
40 summers as a guest of the MacDowell Colony at Peterborough
and you can't help but be absorbed by the New Hampshire
quality.

"How would I define that? Why, it's independence, understatement
– a dry, humorous sense, and, within the walls of the home, a
45 wonderful, congenial homeliness. Lacking in warmth? Not if you
know the idiom.

"I used to think about them on the evening walks of twelve
summers. There are others I know better, but this is basically a
generalization, and it is hard to generalize about one's neighbors.

50 "I wanted to pile up a million details of daily living, with some
sense of the whole in living and dying – San Luis Rey, if you
please. I think it the business of writing to restore that sense of
the whole."

Does Mr. Wilder contemplate a return to teaching (his last
55 assignment, five years as professor of comparative literature,
University of Chicago), or to the novel?

"I should like to think," he replied, gravely, "that after this summer
in which I learned regular work, in extreme retirement, and found
myself completely absorbed in the composition of three plays, I
60 should find myself occupied in the theater for a good number of
years."

Wilder's Own Voice: A Preface

Possibly at the request of Brooks Atkinson, Wilder published "A Preface
for *Our Town*" in the *New York Times* on February 13, 1938. The play
was now safely lodged in the Morosco Theatre when he wrote the
65 Preface. Throughout his life Wilder referred to the formative experience
he had encountered studying archaeology in Rome in 1920–1921,

---

2 **a trifle**: a little   3 **capacious**: large   5 **tapered**: (here) that get thinner towards
the point of the finger

especially its impact on his sense of time, as he reveals in this extract
from his Preface. To it is appended a letter he wrote from Rome to his
family. (This Preface was subsequently forgotten and first appeared back
in print in *American Characteristics*, a collection of Wilder's nonfiction
published in 1979.)   5

For a while in Rome I lived among archeologists, and ever since I
find myself occasionally looking at the things about me as an
archeologist will look at them a thousand years hence. Rockefeller
Center will be reconstructed in imagination from the ruins of its
foundations. How high was it? A thesis will be written on the   10
bronze plates found in New York's detritus heaps – "Tradesmen's
Entrance," "Night Bell."

In Rome I was led through a study of the plumbing on the Palatine
Hill. A friend of mine could ascribe a date, "within ten years," to
every fragment of cement made in the Roman Republic and early   15
Empire.

An archeologist's eyes combine the view of the telescope with the
view of the microscope. He reconstructs the very distant with the
help of the very small.

It was something of this method that I brought to a New   20
Hampshire village. I spent parts of six summers tutoring at Lake
Sunapee and six at the MacDowell Colony at Peterborough. I
took long walks through scores of upland villages.

And the archeologist's and the social historian's points of view
began to mingle with another unremitting preoccupation which   25
is the central theme of the play: What is the relation between the
countless "unimportant" details of our daily life, on the one hand,
and the great perspectives of time, social history, and current
religious ideas, on the other?

What is trivial and what is significant about any one person's   30
making a breakfast, engaging in a domestic quarrel, in a "love
scene," in dying? To record one's feelings about this question is
necessarily to exhibit the realistic detail of life, and one is at once
up against the problem of realism in literature. …

I wished to record a village's life on the stage, with realism and   35
with generality.

The stage has a deceptive advantage over the novel – in that lighted room at the end of the darkened auditorium things seem to be half caught up into generality already. The stage cries aloud
40 its mission to represent the Act in Eternity. So powerful is the focus that it brings to bear on any presented occasion that every lapse of the author from his collaborative intensity is doubly conspicuous: the truth tumbles down into a heap of abject truths and the result is doubly trivial.
45 So I tried to restore significance to the small details of life by removing scenery. The spectator through lending his imagination to the action restages it inside his own head.
In its healthiest ages the theater has always exhibited the least scenery. Aristophanes's *The Clouds* – 423 B.C. Two houses are
50 represented on the stage, inside of one of them we see two beds. Strepsiades is talking in his sleep about his racehorses. A few minutes later he crosses the stage to Socrates's house, the Idea Factory, the "Thinkery." In the Spanish theater Lope de Vega put a rug in the middle of the scene – it was a raft in mid-ocean bearing
55 a castaway. The Elizabethans, the Chinese used similar devices.
The theater longs to represent the symbols of things, not the things themselves. All the lies it tells – the lie that that young lady is Caesar's wife; the lie that people can go through life talking in blank verse; the lie that that man just *killed* that man – all those
60 lies enhance the one truth that is there – the truth that dictated the story, the myth. The theater asks for as many conventions as possible. A convention is an agreed-upon falsehood, an accepted untruth. When the theater pretends to give the real thing in canvas and wood and metal it loses something of the realer thing
65 which is its true business. Ibsen and Chekhov carried realism as far as it could go, and it took all their genius to do it. Now the camera is carrying it on and is in great "theoretical peril" of falling short of literature. (In a world of actual peril that "theoretical

---

11 **detritus** [dɪ'traɪtəs]: rubbish   43 **conspicuous**: easy to see or notice   **abject**: (here) lacking in pride or depth   67 **peril**: danger

peril" looks very farfetched, but ex-college professors must be indulged.)

But the writing of the play was not accompanied by any such conscious argumentation as this. It sprang from a deep admiration for those little white towns in the hills and from a deep devotion to the theater. These are but the belated gropings to reconstruct what may have taken place when the play first presented itself – the life of a village against the life of the stars.

In an earlier draft of the play there were some other lines that led up to those which now serve as its motto. The Stage Manager has been talking about the material that is being placed in the cornerstone of the new bank at Grover's Corners, material that has been chemically treated so that it will last a thousand or two thousand years. He suggests that this play has been placed there so that future ages will know more about the life of the average person; more than just the Treaty of Versailles and the Lindbergh Flight – see what I mean?

Well, people a thousand years from now, in the provinces North of New York at the beginning of the Twentieth Century, people et three times a day – soon after dawn, at noon, and at sunset.

Every seventh day, by law and by religion, there was a day of rest and all work came to a stop.

The religion at that time was Christianity, but I guess you have other records about Christianity.

The domestic set-up was marriage, a binding relation between a male and one female that lasted for life.

... Anything else? Oh, yes, when people died they were buried in the ground just as they were.

Well, people a thousand years from now, this is the way we were – in our growing-up, in our marrying, in our doctoring, in our living, and in our dying.

Now let's get back to our day in Grover's Corners. ...

Thornton Wilder to his family, from Rome, 1921.

I went with an archeological party the other day to a newly discovered tomb of about the first century; it was under a street near the center of the city, and while by candle-light we peered at

faded paintings of a family called Aurelius, symbolic representa-
tions of their dear children and parents borne graciously away by
winged spirits playing in gardens and adjusting their Roman
40 robes, the street cars of today rushed over the loves and pieties
and habits of the Aurelius family, while the same elements were
passing over in Orelio families that will be as great an effort to
recover two thousand years from now, as pleasing an effort, and
as humanizing –

"A Value Above All Price"

45 No line is more quoted in theater programs about *Our Town* than this
sentence from Wilder's 1957 Preface to *Three Plays*. "The play is an
attempt to find a value above all price for the smallest events in our daily
life." Among his papers is his handwritten editorial note on this line,
probably written in the 1960s, and quoted in full below. Did he make
50 this annotation for a reason – perhaps simply for the record? We don't
know. But it is probably Thornton Wilder's last word on what he felt he
had accomplished when he wrote a play called *Our Town*.

The play is an attempt to find a value above all price for the
smallest events in our daily life.
55 But that is absurd. The generations of men follow upon one
another in apparently endless repetition. They are born; they
grow up; they marry; they have children; they die. Where shall
we seek a "value above all price" in these recurrent situations?
The audience in a theatre watches human beings caught up in the
60 happy or unhappy vicissitudes of circumstance. The audience
knows more about what most concerns the characters than they
can ever know themselves. The audience is given a more than
human vision.

---

6 **groping**: (here) attempt to reach for sth.   60 **vicissitudes** (pl): changeable nature
of sth.

In the last act of "Our Town" the author places upon the stage a character who – like the member of the audience – partakes of the "smallest events of our daily life" and is also a spectator of them.

She learns that each life – though it appears to be a repetition among millions – can be felt to be inestimably precious. Though the realization of it is present to us seldom, briefly, and incommunicably. At that moment there are no walls, no chairs, no tables: all is inward. Our true life is the imagination and in the memory.

Information about the Author

In his quiet way, Thornton Niven Wilder was a revolutionary writer who experimented boldly with literary forms and themes, from the beginning to the end of his long career. "Every novel is different from the others," he wrote when he was seventy-five. "The theater (ditto). ... The thing
5 I'm writing now is again totally unlike anything that preceded it." Wilder's richly diverse settings, characters, and themes are at once specific and global. Deeply immersed in classical as well as contemporary literature, he often fused the traditional and the modern in his novels and plays, all the while exploring the cosmic in the commonplace. In a
10 January 12, 1953, cover story, *Time* took note of Wilder's unique "interplanetary mind" – his ability to write from a vision that was at once American and universal.

A pivotal figure in the history of twentieth-century letters, Wilder was a novelist and playwright whose works continue to be widely read and produced in this new century. He is the only writer to have won the Pulitzer Prize for both fiction and drama. His second novel, *The Bridge of San Luis Rey*, received the fiction award in 1928, and he won the prize 5 twice in drama, for *Our Town* in 1938 and *The Skin of Our Teeth* in 1943. His other novels are *The Cabala, The Woman of Andros, Heaven's My Destination, The Ides of March, The Eighth Day*, and *Theophilus North*. His other major dramas include *The Matchmaker*, which was adapted as the internationally acclaimed musical comedy *Hello, Dolly!*, and *The* 10 *Alcestiad*. Among his innovative shorter plays are *The Happy Journey to Trenton and Camden* and *The Long Christmas Dinner*, and two uniquely conceived series, *The Seven Ages of Man* and *The Seven Deadly Sins*, frequently performed by amateurs.

Wilder and his work received many honors, highlighted by the three 15 Pulitzer Prizes, the Gold Medal for fiction from the American Academy of Arts and Letters, the Order of Merit (Peru), the Goethe-Plakette der Stadt Frankfurt am Main (Germany, 1959), the Presidential Medal of Freedom (1963), the National Book Committee's first National Medal for Literature (1965), and the National Book Award for fiction (1967). 20

He was born in Madison, Wisconsin, on April 17, 1897, to Amos Parker Wilder and Isabella Niven Wilder. The family later lived in China and in California, where Wilder was graduated from Berkeley High School. After two years at Oberlin College, he went on to Yale, where he received his undergraduate degree in 1920. A valuable part of his 25 education took place during summers spent working hard on farms in California, Kentucky, Vermont, Connecticut, and Massachusetts. His father arranged these rigorous "shirtsleeve" jobs for Wilder and his older brother, Amos, as part of their initiation into the American experience.

Thornton Wilder studied archaeology and Italian as a special student 30 at the American Academy in Rome (1920–1921), and earned a master of arts degree in French literature at Princeton in 1926.

In addition to his talents as playwright and novelist, Wilder was an accomplished teacher, essayist, translator, scholar, lecturer, librettist, and screenwriter. In 1942, he teamed with Alfred Hitchcock to write the 35 first draft of the screenplay for the classic thriller *Shadow of a Doubt*, receiving credit as principal writer and a special screen credit for his "contribution to the preparation" of the production. All but fluent in four languages, Wilder translated and adapted plays by such varied authors as Henrik Ibsen, Jean-Paul Sartre, and André Obey. As a scholar, he conducted significant research on James Joyce's *Finnegans Wake* and the plays of Spanish dramatist Lope de Vega.

Wilder's friends included a broad spectrum of figures on both sides of the Atlantic – Hemingway, Fitzgerald, Alexander Woollcott, Gene Tunney, Sigmund Freud, producer Max Reinhardt, Katharine Cornell, Ruth Gordon, and Garson Kanin. Beginning in the mid-1930s, Wilder was especially close to Gertrude Stein and became one of her most effective interpreters and champions. Many of Wilder's friendships are documented in his prolific correspondence. Wilder believed that great letters constitute a "great branch of literature." In a lecture entitled "On Reading the Great Letter Writers," he wrote that a letter can function as a "literary exercise," the "profile of a personality," and "news of the soul," apt descriptions of thousands of letters he wrote to his own friends and family.

Wilder enjoyed acting and played major roles in several of his own plays in summer theater productions. He also possessed a lifelong love of music; reading musical scores was a hobby, and he wrote the librettos for two operas based on his work: *The Long Christmas Dinner*, with composer Paul Hindemith, and *The Alcestiad*, with composer Louise Talma. Both works premiered in Germany.

Teaching was one of Wilder's deepest passions. He began his teaching career in 1921 as an instructor in French at Lawrenceville, a private secondary school in New Jersey. Financial independence after the publication of *The Bridge of San Luis Rey* permitted him to leave the classroom in 1928, but he returned to teaching in the 1930s at the University of Chicago. For six years, on a part-time basis, he taught courses there in classics in translation, comparative literature, and composition. In 1950–1951, he served as the Charles Eliot Norton Professor of Poetry at Harvard. Wilder's gifts for scholarship and teaching (he treated the classroom as all but a theater) made him a consummate, much-sought-after lecturer in his own country and abroad. After World

---

34 **librettist**: person who writes librettos (= scripts for operas)

War II, he held special standing, especially in Germany, as an interpreter of his own country's intellectual traditions and their influence on cultural expression.

During World war I, Wilder had served a three-month stint as an enlisted man in the Coast Artillery section of the army, stationed at Fort Adams, Rhode Island. He volunteered for service in World War II, advancing to the rank of lieutenant colonel in Army Air Force Intelligence. For his service in North Africa and Italy, he was awarded the Legion of Merit, the Bronze Star, the Chevalier Legion d'Honneur, and honorary officership in the Military Order of the British Empire (M.B.E.).

From royalties received from *The Bridge of San Luis Rey*, Wilder built a house for his family in 1930 in Hamden, Connecticut, just outside New Haven. But he typically spent as many as two hundred days a year away from Hamden, traveling to and settling in a variety of places that provided the stimulation and solitude he needed for his work. Sometimes his destination was the Arizona desert, the MacDowell Colony in New Hampshire, or Martha's Vineyard, Newport, Saratoga Springs, Vienna, or Baden-Baden. He wrote aboard ships, and often chose to stay in "spas in off-season." He needed as certain refuge when he was deeply immersed in writing a novel or play. Wilder explained his habit to a *New Yorker* journalist in 1959: "The walks, the quiet – all the elegance is present, everything is there but the people. That's it! A spa in off-season! I make a practice of it."

But Wilder always returned to "the house *The Bridge* built," as it is still known to this day. He died there of a heart attack on December 7, 1975.